MAKE MONEY
TRADING OPTIONS

MAKE MONEY
TRADING
OPTIONS

Short-Term Strategies
for Beginners

Michael Sincere

New York   Chicago   San Francisco   Athens   London
Madrid   Mexico City   Milan   New Delhi
Singapore   Sydney   Toronto

2 3 4 5 6 7 8 9   LCR   26 25 24 23 22 21

ISBN   978-1-260-46875-5
MHID   1-260-46875-5

e-ISBN   978-1-260-46876-2
e-MHID   1-260-46876-3

This publication is designed to provide accurate and authoritative information in regard to the subject matter covered. It is sold with the understanding that neither the author nor the publisher is engaged in rendering legal, accounting, securities trading, or other professional services. If legal advice or other expert assistance is required, the services of a competent professional person should be sought.

—From a Declaration of Principles Jointly Adopted by a Committee of the American Bar Association and a Committee of Publishers and Associations

McGraw Hill books are available at special quantity discounts to use as premiums and sales promotions or for use in corporate training programs. To contact a representative, please visit the Contact Us pages at www.mhprofessional.com.

To my wonderful mother and father,
and my amazing dog, Chili.

Contents

Preface

I want to thank you for buying my book, the second in a series that I have written about the options market. Because of the success of my first options book, my editors asked me to write another.

Actually, it was the emails I received from readers that convinced me to write another book. I realized that although readers had been taught how to trade options, they weren't sure how to use what they learned to make money. Thus, this book was created.

This book is aimed at anyone who is relatively new to trading options, but it can also help experienced traders who are looking for new ideas and moneymaking strategies.

Why am I so confident I can show you how to make money trading options? Because I spent over four years evaluating, researching, and studying options strategies until I discovered what works, and what doesn't.

This book is different because it's not based on what I heard or read, but on what I was able to test and verify. I began to think of the stock market as a laboratory, and I was a scientist conducting experiments. Every day, I took detailed notes of what I learned.

From my research, I created a number of moneymaking strategies, but even more important, I learned ways to minimize risk when trading. Making money is not enough—you must know how to protect what you've earned to avoid significant losses.

A Strategy for Almost Everyone

I hope that you approach this book with an open mind and a willingness to accept new ideas. By the time you finish, you may think differently about trading options. Don't get me wrong: I am not saying that the methods I introduce in this book are better than traditional methods. No, they are not better, but they are different.

My goal is to show you multiple techniques for earning money using a variety of strategies, some that are new, and others that are old favorites. I will also reveal a simple and fast way to analyze the stock market that will help regardless of whether you're trading options or stocks.

My research taught me that making bets on which direction a stock or index will move in the future, something that almost everyone else does, is fraught with risk. Unless you are an excellent stock picker, or a fortune-teller, it will be difficult to correctly predict how stocks and indexes will perform.

There is a significant exception, however, and that is when there is a strong bull market. During these wonderful years, anyone who buys *call options* on the strongest and most popular stocks can do well. Unfortunately, bull markets don't last forever, and when they end, so do the profits of many investors.

That is why this book also contains profitable options strategies that work during bear markets. In bear markets, you can still make money, but it's more difficult. And in flat markets, when the market seemingly goes nowhere, you will learn nontraditional options strategies that will help you identify profitable stocks almost every day.

Even though you will learn new ideas, there is no reason to stop using traditional methods, especially if they have worked for you. Many of the ideas introduced in this book should enhance what you already know about the markets.

My plan is to help turn you into a better trader no matter which strategies you are using. As a bonus, I teach you how to reduce risk.

Educate and Entertain

Like my previous books, I wrote this book as if I were having a conversation with you at the kitchen table. However, because I don't want you to lose a lot of money, I will also be as blunt as possible.

I hope to educate and entertain, while showing you how to save time and money. Unfortunately, many traders are woefully unprepared for trading options even after they read books, take classes, or watch videos.

To use an analogy, let's say you wanted to pilot an airplane. Do you think that after reading a few books, watching videos on the internet, or taking a couple of classes, you would be ready to fly? Of course not! It takes a lot more practice and hands-on experience before you would be qualified. It's the same with trading options.

Why I Wrote This Book

Many inexperienced options traders are blissfully unaware of the financial traps that await them before they make that first trade. Except for a few lucky ones, most options traders lose money, perhaps a lot of money, after only a few trading sessions.

Many unsuspecting traders don't realize they are entering a shark-infested arena filled with professionals who are smarter, better trained, and well financed and who are using the most advanced equipment on earth. It's not surprising that so many options traders lose money when making directional trades (betting that a stock or index will go up or down in the future).

I feel it is my responsibility to show you how to earn a profit while also warning you of the many risks that lie in wait. Many traders believe that if they simply choose the right strategy (the more complicated, the better, they think), the more money they will make. That is not necessarily true.

Please don't think that I have all the answers because I don't. Every day, I learn something new while trading options, which I diligently write in my trading notebook. What I can offer, and the reason I wrote this book, is to teach you to trade without risking all or most of your money.

I wish I had a book like this when I first started trading options, and because it didn't exist, I wrote my own. That's right; I wrote a book that even I wanted to read! I believe that sharing what I learned will save you years of wasted time and thousands of dollars in potential losses.

Unfortunately, too many traders rush into the options market with too much money, too little knowledge, and an unrealistic expectation of how much money they can make—all without understanding the risks. Even worse, they often adopt strategies that are too complicated or inappropriate for them.

Even with these obstacles, I want to give you a fighting chance, another reason I wrote this book.

What You Will Learn

I spent a long time researching, analyzing, and experimenting with options, and I want to share my education with you. Here are the three main goals that I want you to achieve as you continue reading:

1. Learn how to minimize risk by avoiding making the common mistakes that doom most options traders.
2. Learn to identify and find winning stocks and ETFs (*exchange-traded funds*) that will bring the most profits.
3. Learn a fast way to evaluate the overall market environment. This will help you decide whether to go long, go short, or not trade at all.

Obviously, you will learn more, but if you can evaluate the overall stock market and find winning stocks almost every day, you will have an edge over other traders.

But let me be clear: Although I am going to teach you ways to make money trading options, it will not be easy, and it won't happen quickly, especially if you're inexperienced. But it is possible, if you are willing to take the time to study, and learn from your mistakes.

How the Book Is Organized

The book is divided into four parts, which can be read in any order. Although you should read each part in full, it's your choice what to read first. Here are the four parts:

- Part One: Managing Risk and Money
- Part Two: The Test Trading Strategy
- Part Three: Other Trading Strategies
- Part Four: The Basics

In Part One, you will learn about risk management, but the information is presented in a different way. Here you will read a fictional story based on the real-life experiences of a hapless options trader, Sam. After the story, I discuss all the mistakes that Sam made, and what he could have done to protect his account.

In Part Two, you will learn about a new method, the Test Trading Strategy, which involves using a simulated or paper trading account to find winning stocks. This easy-to-use, practical strategy is unlike any other options strategy you've read about.

In Part Three you will learn about other options strategies, each designed to make money. Some are new, a few are traditional, and a couple are "off the wall."

In Part Four, beginners who know little about options can take an options minicourse, designed to quickly teach basic options vocabulary and concepts. The minicourse should give enough information about options so that you can read this book without feeling lost. Also, those who know little about technical analysis will be introduced to the two most powerful technical indicators, *moving averages* and RSI (*relative strength index*).

If you are new to options trading, I recommend that you read my first book, the bestselling *Understanding Options*, 2nd edition (McGraw-Hill), which explains in easy-to-understand language how to trade options. Obviously, there are also dozens of other options books available online or at bookstores.

How to Contact Me

Thanks again for taking the time to read my book. Not everyone is willing to try something new, so I appreciate that you're willing to learn different ideas and strategies. As always, I do my best to make this one of the most useful options books you ever read.

My goal is to show you how to make a decent amount of money (a sum that varies for each person) on your own, so you don't have to rely on me or anyone else to be successful. I truly hope that I inspire you to make your own discoveries the same way that I did.

Finally, if you have questions about my book or notice any errors, feel free to email me at msincere@gmail.com, or visit my website, www.michaelsincere.com. I always enjoy hearing from you, and I'll try to answer promptly.

. . . .

Now let's get to work—there is a lot to learn!

MAKE MONEY
TRADING
OPTIONS

PART ONE

MANAGING RISK AND MONEY

As you know from reading the Preface, this book is divided into four parts. To make the process easier, you can read them in any order. In this part, you will learn about managing risk and money. No matter how good the strategy, or how much you know about using options, if you do not successfully manage risk, it will be difficult to retain profits.

There is no way for traders and investors to avoid losing money from time to time. That is expected. But managing risk means keeping losses to a reasonable level. Your ultimate goal is to earn more money than you lose.

Most traders prefer to learn new strategies and think of stock ideas rather than manage risk. Truthfully, it's not that much fun to talk about limiting profits. However, that's exactly what you must do if you plan on making money. If you ignore this important step in your trading education, it will come back to haunt you one day.

In the middle of a trade, there is often little time to do anything other than react to the market. You may not have time to study a list of "what-to-do" rules. If you don't make the right decisions, and quickly, it's possible that you won't survive the day without losses that are larger than you can afford.

You are not reading this book to lose money. As the author, a job I take seriously, I will do everything in my power to help you avoid account-killing losses.

I apologize for being blunt, but if you are unwilling to understand the importance of minimizing risk, you would be better off forgetting about trading options. Instead, find another way to make money that won't be harmful to your portfolio. Consider investing for the long term and not trading.

In reality, the best way to learn how to manage risk is by making trades. That is what you will do in Part Two. As you continue reading, it will be obvious that risk management is more than memorizing a list of rules. Instead, it's something you must continuously practice and experience for yourself by making buy, hold, or sell decisions.

In the real world, one of the best ways to understand risk is to lose money, but hopefully not much. I'm sure you know the classic children's lesson: You tell a child a dozen times not to touch a hot stove. Like most curious children, one day the child will ignore your advice and touch the stove. Guess what? That will be the last time that will happen!

The first, and most important, risk management lesson is this: Learn to trade small position size, which means not risking large sums of money. After you've been properly trained, there will be plenty of time for you to increase the amount of money you place at risk with each trade.

One more thing: Although you will learn ways to reduce risk, you can never eliminate risk completely. There is always a chance that the trade will not go as planned. Perhaps you will make a mistake and buy an option at the wrong time and at the wrong price. If that happens, you are bound to lose money, but with proper risk management, the losses won't be devastating.

Your first job as a trader is to avoid large losses. Next, you must improve your trading skills. And finally, you will work on making money. If you keep risk under control, and if you have some trading skills, you should be able to earn profits.

Similar to touching a hot stove, losing money is one of the best ways to learn what not to do. The trick is to lose small by cutting losses when the trade is not performing as anticipated, and to collect bigger profits when you own a winning position. If you can accomplish that, then you will have made great progress in your trading education.

Finally, don't think that I have all the answers, because I don't. Every day I learn something new about the ever-changing stock market. What I can do, however, is show you ways to trade not just for a day, but for a lifetime.

Managing Risk

It's a challenge to teach others how to manage risk. The traditional method is to present advice or a list of rules such as these: "Be disciplined." "Don't lose money." "Buy low, sell high." These rules are often so general that they are nearly worthless.

Even more important, how can you learn about the pitfalls and traps you may face as a trader without being bored? That's when I thought of a novel way to teach you about risk management.

If you are willing to spend a few minutes to read an educational but entertaining story about the real-life experiences of an options trader, you should gain some valuable insights. At the conclusion of the story, we will analyze all the mistakes the options trader made, and the lessons learned.

I know there may be readers who want to skip the story and lessons and go directly to Chapter 3, where you learn moneymaking strategies. If you do skip this chapter, be sure that you return at some point. Managing risk is essential to your trading success—you don't want to trade without it.

And now, for those who want to learn about the many ways you can lose money during the trading day, and what to do about it, keep reading. You may find that your emotions, besides the market itself, are your biggest opponent. That is always a challenge for every trader.

I hope you enjoy this fictional story based on the real-life experiences of one hapless options trader. For fun, see if you can identify all the mistakes that Sam made in one week. We'll discuss those errors in Chapter 2.

Note: If you are not familiar with options vocabulary, you may want to go to Chapter 10 and read the options mini-course first before reading the story.

1

A Week in the Life of an Options Trader

Sam was a middle-aged retired teacher who had invested most of his money in an IRA account. He had 60 percent of his money in stocks and index funds and 40 percent invested in bonds. Sam wanted to find a way to increase his income while also having something to do. Retirement was already boring.

It was Sam's young nephew who suggested that he consider trading options. His nephew was making big profits trading options from home, and he finally convinced Sam to try it out for himself.

Sam began by reading a book on trading options. Then he watched online videos on how to make money trading. After a few weeks of studying, Sam felt he was ready to trade with real money. He also spoke about options with his neighbor Bradley, who had been trading stocks and options for years. Bradley often shared his success stories.

After much thought, Sam decided to begin by purchasing *calls* and *puts*, one of the most basic options strategies. Sam didn't feel ready to try the complicated strategies his nephew used. He wanted to keep it simple.

Sam decided to trade using money in his IRA account because he wanted all taxes on his earnings to be deferred. He spoke to a representative at the brokerage firm to be certain that his trading would be allowed in a retirement account. The broker told Sam that buying calls and puts was allowed.

Sam told the broker to sell his stocks and mutual funds so he could trade options. "I want to make a lot of money," Sam told the broker. Because Sam had almost $150,000 in his account, he was free to make as many trades as he liked, including trading daily, trading weekly, or holding even longer.

In reality, Sam had no idea how to choose an option or how long to hold a position. With stocks, he just bought and almost never sold. "Maybe it's different with options," he said to his broker.

"It is very different," the broker said, nodding. "Read this first." The broker handed him a thick brochure called "Characteristics and Risks of Standardized Options."

When Sam arrived home, he put the brochure in a drawer with no plans to read it.

Monday Morning

On Monday morning, August 3, Sam was eager to make his first options trade. He set up his computer and two iPads for trading. Sam had no idea what he should buy, so he turned on the TV to a financial program to get stock ideas.

After watching for 20 minutes, he wrote down the names of stocks the touts on the program had recommended. The one stock that everyone on the show liked was Apple, which was reporting its quarterly earnings in two days.

Sam thought that buying Apple was a great idea. Apple was a successful company that Sam knew well. It seemed like a no-brainer:

Buy call options on Apple before earnings were announced and make money when the stock price rose. It didn't hurt that Apple stock had been rising for weeks. "I may as well join the party," he thought.

Sam had already opened his brokerage account and was ready to place an order to buy 10 calls on Apple at its current price. Anxious to get started, he had to wait until the options market opened at 9:30 a.m.

The futures market was pointing to a lower opening. It appeared as if the Dow was going to drop by almost 1 percent at the open, a 240-point fall. The Standard and Poor's 500 index (S&P 500, or SPX) was also down by 1 percent. Sam was glad because he could buy his Apple calls at a lower price. Buy low, sell high was the number one rule that he had always been told.

Sam was also thinking that since the market was going to fall at the open, maybe he should take advantage of the market decline and buy puts on the indexes. He knew from reading that one way to make that bet is to buy puts on SPY, a popular ETF that tracked the S&P 500.

As soon as the market opened at 9:30 a.m. ET, Sam made his decision. He immediately placed a *limit order* to buy 10 Apple calls (September 18 at-the-money strike price). The bid and ask prices were $21.85 × $22.40, and Sam's limit price was $22.40. The total cost of the trade would be $22,400.

Sam thought it was a little expensive, but after all, Apple was an expensive stock. "You have to pay to play," Sam thought. Sam figured that he wasn't the only one who wanted to buy Apple calls, which is why they were so expensive.

Sam knew from reading his trading books that his primary goal was not to lose money. That was why he bought only 10 Apple calls (at the money) even though he thought of buying more.

"I'm buying options on one of the most popular stocks in the world," Sam reminded himself.

Only minutes after the market opened, Apple bucked the market downtrend and moved up so quickly that Sam's limit order wasn't immediately filled. That really annoyed Sam, as he expected to buy it for $22.40 per contract. He went back to the order screen and saw that the ask price for Apple had risen to $23.95. It was on its way higher because Apple, the *underlying stock*, was moving higher. The cost of call options increased as the stock price increased.

To make sure he got his order filled this time, Sam broke one of the rules he had read about in the books. The authors always said to only place a limit order, not a market order. But if he used a limit order, Sam thought, his order might not get filled immediately. He didn't want to miss out on buying these calls.

Sam ignored the advice from the books and placed a market order to buy 10 Apple calls (at the money). His order was filled at $24.65, the highest price of the day so far, but Sam was thankful he owned those calls. The cost was $24,650.

Ten minutes after he bought those options, Sam looked at his account and saw he was already up by $720. "Wow," Sam thought. "This is easy."

A few minutes later, the Dow began to falter. It was now down by 312 points, a 1.3 percent drop. The S&P 500 was down by almost 1.4 percent. Sam was annoyed that he didn't buy those SPY puts, which would have been profitable.

As the stock indexes moved lower, Sam felt nervous. When the Dow had fallen by 340 points, and the S&P 500 kept dropping, he was unable to stand it any longer. He placed a new order to buy 10 SPY puts (September at-the-money puts with a bid-ask price of $13.65 × $13.69). "This is expensive," Sam thought, but not as expensive as the Apple calls.

He was anxious to get his order filled, so he placed a market order to buy, even though he knew he should have placed a limit order. "No time to waste," Sam thought to himself. Most important to Sam, if the market continued to fall, the puts would make money.

His order for the SPY puts was filled at $13.71. The total cost of the order was $13,710.

Sam had no comprehension of how options decayed on a daily basis, but he liked the idea of owning both puts and calls. The only problem was that his Apple calls were slowly falling lower with the market. It was annoying that he was now only up by $320 on the Apple calls. Fortunately, his SPY puts were up by $110.

Sam looked at his IRA account. He had spent almost $38,000 on only two positions.

While Sam wondered what to do next, his cell phone rang. His neighbor Bradley yelled into the phone: "The market's going to crash! This is the big one!"

"How do you know?" Sam asked.

"I just know!" Bradley snapped. "I have never been more certain of anything in my life. Sell short, buy puts; this is a crash!"

"I'll think about it," Sam said, but Bradley had already hung up.

Sam considered Bradley as a know-it-all who bragged about how much money he had made in the market. Bradley often got emotional when the market made extreme moves, and sure enough, he was emotional.

Sam looked at the quotes on the Dow and S&P 500 and saw that the market was still falling, but not as quickly as before. He glanced at the chart and saw a downtrend. "Maybe Bradley was right," Sam thought.

Sam didn't want to miss out on a put-buying opportunity if the market was going to crash, so he returned to the brokerage order screen and placed a limit order to buy an additional 10 SPY puts (September at the money). Sam's heart was racing as he placed the order, afraid he was going to miss making money from the coming crash.

He looked at his screen and saw he had paid $15.10. Sam now owned 20 SPY puts.

As the market continued to fall, *implied volatility* rose, and the price of those puts increased in value even more quickly than he had thought possible. Sam didn't care about any of that. He was glad he had bought those puts before they went any higher.

Sam looked at the position page on his brokerage account: His Apple calls had turned from a winner to a $235 loser. Fortunately, his SPY puts had gained in value, and he was ahead by $1,855.

"If I sell now," Sam thought, "I could make a profit of $1,620." Sam looked at the clock. "$1,620 profit in only 30 minutes! This is great."

Sam had no intention of selling, because if the market really crashed, he could make a small fortune on those SPY puts. And, he thought, Apple wasn't going to fall that much. "No," Sam told himself, "I'm holding."

Although Sam had high hopes for Apple, the stock continued to fall with the market. When he looked, his Apple position was a $880 loser. "Hmmm, that's not good," he thought. Luckily, the SPY puts were still in the black and gaining in value.

Sam remembered the golden rule of trading: "Cut your losses. Hold your winners." It was drilled into the head of every trader. Because Apple went from a winner to a loser, Sam decided to sell his Apple calls and take the loss. It wasn't a hard decision, especially when he was doing so well with the SPY puts. He decided to sell his entire Apple position.

Sam placed a limit order to sell the 10 Apple calls. He wished he had time to negotiate a better price, perhaps between the bid and ask price, but he was in a rush. He didn't want to lose any more money.

Sam noticed that the order wasn't filled immediately because the Apple calls were rapidly losing value. He canceled, then placed the order again until he got filled at $23.20. He had lost $1,450 on the position.

The 20 SPY puts were still up since Sam had bought them. Minutes earlier, he had a profit of $1,620 in his account, and now the gains had declined because of those Apple calls.

To add to his misery and confusion, the Dow and SPX had stopped falling. "I went from a $1,620 gain to almost nothing," Sam thought. "I wish I had sold earlier. But I'll get my money back."

Sam wanted to recover the losses from his Apple trade, so he decided to add to his SPY puts. He remembered reading that you should add to your winners, and his SPY puts were winning. "I am just following the rules," he told himself.

Sam placed a limit order to buy an additional 10 SPY puts (September at the money), which was filled. He now owned a total of 30 SPY puts, and the market was moving sideways. His puts were now losing value despite the sideways market. Once again, this was because of implied volatility, which was working against Sam.

Leaving his trading screen to go to his kitchen, Sam opened the refrigerator to get a bite to eat. All that trading made him hungry.

Return from Morning Snack

Ten minutes later, when Sam walked back to his computer, he noticed that the 30 SPY puts had lost value. Before, he was up by $1,855. Now he was only up by only $1,100. With the $1,450 loss on the Apple calls, his account was now in the red.

While he watched his SPY puts, Sam looked at other stocks. He noticed that even though the overall market was lower, Tesla was up by 0.83 percent. He thought about buying Tesla calls, but he passed on the idea because the overall market was so weak. Sam also thought about buying Microsoft, but it wasn't exciting enough. He liked fast-moving stocks.

Sam was surprised to see Apple reverse direction and move higher. He might have lost only a little money if he had waited only 10 minutes longer. It annoyed him how Apple moved higher right after he sold it.

Sam still thought the market was going to move lower, so he waited. He held his 30 SPY puts and had no thoughts of selling until he was proved right.

He was still irritated that Apple moved higher all morning. When he couldn't stand the idea that he had made a bad trade, Sam rebought the 10 Apple calls (September at the money) using a limit order. He knew he was chasing after Apple, but he didn't care. He didn't want to miss out as Apple rose. Even though the market was down all morning, Apple had reversed and continued to rally. "I never should have sold those calls," he mumbled to himself.

Sam now owned 30 SPY puts and 10 Apple calls. As the market went higher, his SPY put gains rapidly disappeared. He didn't want to look at how much he had lost. More importantly, he never considered how much money he had spent on options, and now he had a negative balance.

"I'll make it back," he promised himself.

Monday Midday (12 Noon ET)

Sam noticed that Tesla was also trading with the market trend. As the Dow and S&P 500 went higher, so did Apple and Tesla. Sam opened his trading screen and saw that Tesla calls were priced at $154 per contract. Even buying one call contract of Tesla would cost $15,400. "That's a little too rich for my blood," Sam mumbled.

Fifteen minutes later, as the market moved sideways, Sam watched as Tesla went even higher. He couldn't stand losing money on a trade he had missed, so he impulsively bought one Tesla call (September at the money). The final cost was $15,530.

Sam was worried because he had used three-quarters of his retirement savings to make these trades. But then he thought about the profits he'd make if his market view turned out to be correct. He dismissed his concerns and focused on his account balance.

His IRA account balance had dropped to $147,500. He was holding almost $80,000 in options.

Sam was upset that minutes after buying Tesla calls, he was already losing $460. He didn't know what he had done wrong. He remembered that many traders liked Tesla, and that it had made some wealthy. Anyway, he had only bought one call, although it was costly.

Sam looked at his position page: He owned 30 SPY puts, 10 Apple calls, and 1 Tesla call. He thought he was in a good position to make a lot of money. He had both long positions (calls) that would prosper in a rising market and short positions (puts) that would do well on a market decline.

Although Sam had only three option positions, he was anxious. He couldn't imagine holding any more positions than this. Just watching three positions was nerve-racking. He had heard of day traders who held dozens of stock and option positions. "I don't know how they do it," he thought.

Sam watched as the value of his portfolio changed rapidly during lunch. He was still underwater on those original Apple calls, and his SPY puts were struggling. The Tesla calls were also in the red, but not by much. He was too nervous to eat lunch.

Sam saw that the market was slowly moving higher. Minutes ago, the Dow was down by 127 points, and now the decline was only 89 points. The 10 Apple calls had gained value with the market. Unfortunately, the 30 SPY puts were now losing money. The Tesla calls hardly moved at all.

Lost and Confused

Sam felt uncomfortable. The Dow and S&P 500 continued to erase their losses, so his 30 SPY puts were sinking. The Apple and Tesla calls had gained, but not by a huge amount. It was the SPY position that caused the most pain. He was down by $4,600 on the SPY puts. He had bought too many and at terrible prices.

"This is a disaster," Sam thought. He wished he hadn't bought those SPY puts.

Sam thought about selling all three positions, but that would be a $5,600 loss. "How could I lose that much money?" he thought.

The market continued to rise as the value of his SPY puts declined. Although he didn't know it, implied volatility was getting crushed, adding to his woes. The implied volatility decline reduced the value of both his calls and puts.

As the Dow continued to rise, Sam looked at his account. He was now down by over $6,700 on those 30 SPY puts. For the first time all day, Sam felt fear. The stronger the rally, the more money he lost. The Apple and Tesla calls were not earning money as fast as the SPY puts were falling.

It had never occurred to Sam that he could lose that much money so quickly.

While he was thinking what to do, Bradley called again. "Hey," Bradley said. "Trust me. Buy more puts."

"I'm already losing money on the puts you told me to buy."

"Don't be dumb," Bradley said. "It's time to plunge!" He hung up.

Sam wondered if his neighbor was right. Bradley knew a lot more about the stock market than he did. Sam already owned 30 SPY puts that had lost money. Just in case Bradley was right, Sam bought five more SPY puts (September at the money). "After this, I'm not buying anymore puts," Sam promised himself.

After the limit order was filled, the indexes continued to rise. The Dow was now in the green by 12 points. Immediately, Sam had lost money on the new puts. He kicked himself again. He remembered reading that you should never add to losers, and that's exactly what he had done. "Why did I do that?" he wondered.

Monday Afternoon

In one day, Sam was already down by $8,200, and he was furious. He had worked his whole life to accumulate this money, and it was going away far too quickly. He was especially frustrated that he had a gain of $1,620 that morning but let it get away. He felt light-headed.

The only good news was the 10 Apple calls had risen and showed a profit of more than $1,400. The Tesla call was also higher by $932. But Sam's losses on the SPY puts were almost $10,000. He owned too many puts, and the market was still rising. If he sold all his positions now, he would have a huge loss.

As the Dow trended higher, Sam was tempted to sell all 35 puts if the market continued in the same direction. Sam was stymied because he had no plan other than try to get his money back. His put options were too painful to watch, so he didn't.

The market meandered back and forth until 2:00 p.m. ET with very little action. The gains in Tesla and Apple were decent, more than $1,800 combined, but the loss from his SPY puts was devastating.

The market moved so slowly during the afternoon that it almost put Sam to sleep. He had thought trading would be fun, but this wasn't fun at all.

The Dow was now up by 54 points. Sam had a $2,100 gain in the Tesla and Apple calls, but as the indexes climb higher, he kept losing on those puts.

He had no intention of holding a losing position overnight. That's one rule he remembered. Holding 35 puts overnight would be too risky and dangerous, and there was no way he could sleep at night if he did. He looked at his account balance. He had lost a total of almost $11,500, all in one day.

With the market set to close in 15 minutes, Sam made a decision. He sold 25 of his SPY puts, leaving him holding 10 puts. If the market fell tomorrow morning, his puts would make money. If the market rose, his Tesla and Apple calls would make money. It seemed like a reasonable plan.

Sam glanced at his position page and was stunned to see that he had lost almost $13,000, mostly because of those stupid SPY puts. He was lucky he had kept those Apple and Tesla calls. He also wished he had never listened to Bradley.

Sam left his house for the first time all day. He didn't want to think about the market until tomorrow. It wasn't fun to sit in front of the computer all day, especially when losing money. He still wished he had taken the profit when he had the chance. He vowed to trade differently tomorrow.

Tuesday Morning

When the market opened at 9:30 a.m. ET, the Dow spiked higher by more than 236 points. Sam was upset that his 10 SPY puts got crushed, with additional losses of almost $1,200. His Apple and Tesla calls had gained almost $1,700, but he was still down (both financially and emotionally) on those SPY puts.

Sam couldn't take the pain anymore, so he sold all 10 SPY puts and locked in the loss. He had lost a total of more than $16,000 on all the SPY puts, but at least he had stopped the bleeding. The Dow was still up by 220 points.

Now Sam hoped the market would rally all day. Maybe he could make back the awful losses from the SPY puts.

10:00 A.M. ET Reversal

Around 10:15 a.m., the market stalled and fell a little lower. When Sam looked, the Dow was higher by only 155 points. Sam looked at his one Tesla call, which was deep in the loss column. "What?" he said to himself. "Why did that happen?"

He was angry because he thought he had done everything right but he was losing money. He had sold his losers like he was taught and held his winners. Unfortunately, everything reversed direction.

The Dow continued to fall. His Apple calls were still profitable by $2,100, but his one Tesla call had sold off strongly, resulting in a current loss of almost $2,800. "How could I lose this much money?" Sam wondered. "I only owned one call!"

Sam refused to lose any more money on the Tesla call, so he frantically opened the trade screen and placed a limit order to sell. He wanted out of the position.

After the order was filled, Sam looked at the position page. His loss on Tesla was $4,700. He couldn't believe his bad luck. He was down more than $20,000 in his IRA account, a loss of almost 12 percent. "I've never lost that much money in my life!" he moaned.

Sam vowed not to trade for the rest of the day. He felt so stupid losing that much money so quickly. He would try again on Wednesday morning.

Now he only had one position, and that was 10 Apple calls. The good news, Sam thought, was that Apple was reporting earnings tomorrow after the close. He could make back all his lost money with one good trade.

He left his house and didn't look at the market for the rest of the day. While riding his bicycle, he went over some of the mistakes he had made in his mind. "Maybe I'm a terrible trader," he thought. "I bought and sold everything at the wrong time."

Wednesday Morning

Sam's only plan was to hold the 10 Apple calls all day and then wait for Apple to report its earnings. Before the market opened, he watched the financial shows. He was glad that everyone was bullish on Apple.

He was still in disbelief that he had lost more than $20,000 in two days and vowed to trade better. He checked the futures market and was pleased to see that the market was going to rally at the start of the trading day. That was a good omen for his Apple calls.

He also noticed that Tesla had rallied back from yesterday and was higher by 6 percent in the premarket. He was angry with himself for selling the Tesla call so early. He could have made back some of his money, but it was too late now. That was yesterday. Today was a new day.

Now, everything depended on Apple and its earnings.

As soon as the market opened, the Dow and SPX rose by more than 1.2 percent. "I'm glad I sold those SPY puts," Sam thought.

He had a decent gain of $3,200 on the Apple calls. That helped to soothe some of the pain he felt.

Wednesday Midday: The Boy Plunger

Sam had no intention of trading on Wednesday but changed his mind when the Dow, and Apple, rallied higher at midday. Apple had risen by more than 2 percent, and if it kept climbing, he could recover some of what he had lost on the SPY puts. The annoying part was that Tesla was up over 9 percent. If he hadn't sold Tesla, he would have been in better shape.

The market continued to rise. Sam was certain it would keep going higher. He was finished with the put buying experiment. The market was too strong.

Sam was anxious to earn enough to cover his losses. He was sure that if he plunged into the market with Apple calls, he could make it all back.

All of the analysts said that Apple's earnings were going to be fantastic. If Apple beat the earnings estimates, Apple stock would go to the moon, and so would the call options. "This is a can't-lose play," Sam thought.

Sam's calls were trading higher, and he was thrilled. At the rate that Apple was rising, he might even have a profit by the end of the day. Apple was 3 percent higher for the day. It was trading at $402 per share.

Although Sam had vowed to not buy too many options, he needed to make some of his money back. The Dow and Nasdaq were on a roll, and Sam was not going to be left behind.

He placed an order to buy 20 more calls on Apple at a limit price of $16.10 at the 400 strike price. He chose an expiration date that was only three weeks away to save money. He paid $32,200 for the calls.

The price of the options had climbed all morning as implied volatility rose, and as more traders bid the stock higher. It was obvious to Sam he wasn't the only one clamoring for Apple options.

Sam was certain he was right in his expectations. In a worst-case scenario, even if Apple declined by a small amount the next day, it had always come back in the past. Sam spent the rest of the day reading about how everyone was predicting Apple would beat its earnings estimates.

Sam felt awful when he looked at his account balance. He was down by more than $18,000. He hoped that Apple would save him.

Wednesday Afternoon

With 30 calls, equivalent to 3,000 shares of Apple stock, Sam watched as Apple went up and down like a roller coaster all day. He realized that he had bought Apple near the high of the day, but it didn't matter. He couldn't wait until the end of the day when Apple reported its earnings.

In the afternoon, Apple had fallen back a little. It didn't bother Sam because he was 100 percent sure Apple would beat the predicted earnings.

Apple Reports Earnings

Minutes after the market closed, Apple announced the news. As everyone predicted, the earnings were fantastic, and Apple exceeded analysts' expectations. Sam felt great about the good news, and he was excited about tomorrow's opening price so he could cash in his winning options.

As he listened to the earnings announcement, he noticed that the report wasn't perfect. Although Apple had an excellent quarter, the company also mentioned that it was unsure about future sales, and so could not guarantee that iPhone sales would continue at the same breakneck pace as that of the current quarter.

Sam's heart sank when the stunned host said that Apple stock was selling off hard in after-hours trading. "The earnings were perfect," the host said with a surprised look. "But the market didn't like it."

Sam looked at Apple's stock. It was down 7 percent in after-hours trading. Seven percent! "I'm ruined!" Sam yelled at himself. He threw one of his iPads against the wall, cracking its screen.

Sam was so scared he couldn't think straight. If Apple opened 7 percent lower, he could lose another $10,000. Then he calmed down as he remembered how Apple always came back after any sell-off.

"I'm not going to panic. I'm not going to panic," he said repeatedly. He tried to convince himself that his losses were not as bad as they seemed.

Sam wished he had selected a longer expiration date, because three weeks might not be enough time for Apple to bounce back.

Since he owned options, Apple had to move in the right direction within three weeks.

Sam didn't sleep well that night and woke up at 5:00 a.m., hoping against hope that Apple had recovered. He was demoralized to discover it had fallen even further in overnight trading as risk-averse institutions sold shares of their stock.

Every tout on the television shows talked about Apple and how it had beat its earnings but was still falling after hours.

"This is not fair," Sam mumbled at the TV.

Thursday Morning

At 9:25 a.m. ET, five minutes before the market opened, Sam devised a plan. No matter what happened, he was going to hold his Apple calls for one week. He was certain that other buyers would enter the market and buy Apple at a discounted price. It happened before, and it would happen again.

The Apple news caused the indexes to open lower at 9:30 a.m. ET. Nasdaq was falling even more than the Dow or S&P 500. Investors worried that if Apple expected a bad quarter in its future, maybe other companies would, too.

While the Dow opened lower by 75 points, the Nasdaq 100, which primarily consists of technology stocks, got slammed. It was down by 2.3 percent.

Sam didn't want to look at his trading screen after the market opened. The market was a little lower, but Apple got smashed by 8 percent and was declining further. Sam was now down by over $4,000 in one day as the price of his 30 calls kept falling.

When Sam saw that he had lost more than $25,000 in his IRA account, he turned off his trading screen. He left the house, went shopping, and glanced at his phone a couple of times. Nasdaq and the other indexes continued to fall all afternoon.

Thursday Afternoon

When Sam returned to his computer, he saw he had losses of nearly $28,000. Instead of bouncing back, Apple continued to sink as nervous investors were selling Apple and other technology companies.

The Nasdaq was 3.5 percent lower. Sam wished he had held those SPY puts. He had no idea what to do next.

He got a call from Bradley. "I told you to buy puts!" Bradley yelled into the phone. "I hope you followed my advice."

"Not really," Sam said in a meek voice.

"Are you crazy? You should have listened to me."

"I have to go," Sam said, and hung up.

Sam was too frightened to do anything. He was certain that Apple would recover, but obviously not today. Sam remembered reading that panic and fear don't last long. Soon, he hoped, investors looking for a bargain would step in and buy Apple shares.

The market continued to fall right into the close. That's when a large seller decided to dump its holdings, and Apple plunged again with a minute left in the trading day.

Sam looked at his trading screen and saw that he had lost nearly $36,000. "It's only a paper loss," he told himself. "It's not a real loss until I sell."

His IRA account was down by over 24 percent.

Friday Morning

In the middle of the night, Sam was horrified to see that the futures market was moving lower. He was sure that the market was going to bounce back, but not right away. Worse for Sam, in after-hours trading, Apple was down by another 2 percent. Sam just couldn't believe his bad luck.

When the market opened the next day, Apple continued to fall. It didn't really matter because Sam had already lost most of his money on the position. Now Sam was panicked. This was his life's savings!

He just couldn't take the pain any longer. He waited a few minutes to see if Apple would bounce back, but it didn't. Apple continued to fall after the opening bell. He had no hope of getting his money back, so he sold all 30 Apple calls.

After he sold, Sam sat in his chair in disbelief. "This is a nightmare," he thought. He was shocked that he could lose almost $40,000 in just a few days.

Sam went from shock to anger. He wanted to know who took his money. He was so furious he thought of never buying options again.

He sat in his chair and stared at the wall. His retirement account had been shredded. Now he would have to look for a job.

· · · · · · · · ·

Now that you've finished reading about Sam's disastrous week, in Chapter 2 we will discuss all the mistakes that Sam made, and the lessons he should have learned.

2

Lessons Learned the Hard Way

Perhaps you think that no trader would ever make as many mistakes as Sam, but in fact, it happens, although hopefully not in one week. It's common for everyone to make trading mistakes, but this is especially true for new traders when money is on the line.

The sum that Sam lost is not as important as the percentage of the trading account that he squandered, which in Sam's case had risen to 27 percent.

Regardless of the amount you have to lose before it's a disaster (and that sum differs for each trader), be aware of how much money you place at risk for any single trade. Knowing and managing that amount is the number one risk management tool.

Establish a maximum possible loss for any trade, and make it a sum that you will be unhappy to lose, but is one that you can afford without severe financial harm.

If Sam had managed his money and risk properly, traded much smaller position size, and used fewer dollars until he had gained more experience, he could have avoided making so many mistakes. Losing so much money was a deadly error that never should have happened.

Of all the lessons you may have learned from Sam, here is the most important: *Trade small.* Trading small has two meanings. First, trade with a minimum number of contracts. Second, keep your options trading account small no matter how much money you have.

If Sam had followed this one rule, he would have avoided the biggest hits to his account. The purpose of trading small size is to limit the amount of money at risk, especially when first getting started. Sam had no business holding so many contracts, especially when the options were so expensive. The kind of trades that Sam was making could bankrupt him in days. Of course, it ended in tears and frustration.

Below is a brief explanation of all the errors that Sam made, and the lessons he should have learned. The goal is to avoid making the same mistakes that he did. I don't expect you to remember all these lessons at one time, so plan to revisit this section again in the future. When you are ready to begin trading, and before too much money is at risk, it will be worthwhile to review these lessons. Remember the ones that are meaningful to you.

Unfortunately, everyone makes mistakes when first starting out, and you will, too. The goal is to keep those mistakes to a minimum. Most importantly, try not to keep repeating the same mistakes.

And now, here is a brief analysis of Sam's disastrous week as an options trader.

The Lessons

1. The first mistake was that Sam had no plan or strategy to follow. Because he had no buying or selling strategies, he was trading by the seat of his pants without a clue when to buy or sell. At a minimum, he should have created price tar-

gets and profit targets. (We'll discuss this more thoroughly later in the book.) *Lesson: Create a trading plan, script, or strategy before the market opens, and follow it.*

2. As mentioned earlier, but worth repeating: Sam didn't pay any attention to how much money was invested in each trade. In other words, he didn't trade small. Instead of buying 1 or 2 contracts, or setting a dollar limit per trade, Sam went all in with 10, then 20 expensive calls, until he was holding as many as 40 option contracts. By that time, he was in way over his head. *Lesson: Trade small until you gain confidence and experience.*

3. Sam got his stock ideas from TV, the internet, or suggestions from his friend. Sam should have had the patience to create a stock list based on his own criteria. He should not have bought options just because Bradley told him to do so. *Lesson: Don't get your trade ideas from tipsters. Find your own stocks.*

4. Sam appeared to make decisions based on greed, a common emotion when trading. One of the worst outcomes for new traders is earning a quick profit. That leads to overconfidence and a belief that trading is easy. In turn, that leads to risking larger and larger sums. Soon, they are trading way more contracts (and cash) than is reasonable or prudent. *Lesson: Recognize feelings of greed, and stop trading until those feelings go away.*

5. Although owning three positions might not seem like a lot of positions to manage, it was for Sam. A novice trader like Sam should have no more than one position until he is certain he can handle another. That comes with risk management experience. Perhaps some traders can juggle multiple positions, but wait until you can successfully handle one or two positions. *Lesson: Don't own too many positions at one time.*

6. Even though Sam was faced with huge losses, he continued to increase, not reduce, the number of trades he made. Adding new positions and increasing the size of existing positions led to a terrible conclusion. The solution in this situation would be to trade less often, and with fewer contracts. *Lesson: Don't overtrade.*

7. If Sam had traded with fewer contracts, and had less cash at risk, it would have solved many of his problems. But by the time he owned a 40-lot position, he was out of control. Trading smaller and less often would have decreased his emotions, leading to fewer losses. He should not have owned a position where the maximum theoretical loss would be painful. *Lesson: Trade small, trade less, and manage emotions.*

8. Sam knew the trading guidelines about cutting losses and holding winners, but the rules are not written in stone. Although these are good suggestions for traders, and serve an important purpose, there are times when you have to break the rules. Sam followed the guidelines but lost money. *Lesson: Be flexible when trading.*

9. With options (and stocks), morning profits can turn into afternoon losses, as it did for Sam, who watched as his $1,620 gain turned into a loss. There is nothing more frustrating and worse for a trader's ego than seeing a winner turn into a loser. Or as I like to say: You go to sleep as a king and wake up as a peasant. To reduce the chances that this will happen to you, watch positions closely. This is one of the most difficult aspects of trading because it's nearly impossible to predict which option positions will gain in value and which will become losers. *Lesson: Look for an opportunity to sell big winners.*

10. Sam was in such a rush to buy options that he placed market orders, getting poor prices. He should have taken the

time to negotiate for better prices. There is usually no reason that you must make a trade "right now." Sometimes it's okay to miss a trade. *Lessons: In the trading world, only fools rush in. Use limit orders, and don't trade if you are panicked or overly emotional.*

11. It should be obvious that Sam never should have listened to the advice from Bradley. It's wise not to receive phone calls or text messages when you are in the middle of a trade. If your friends want to give advice, tell them to call when the market is closed. *Lesson: Don't accept phone calls or text messages while trading.*

12. Sam was not only betting big with options, but speculating with his retirement money. It turned out to be a disaster. By tapping into his IRA, he put his retirement at risk. That was a mistake, all because he wanted to defer taxes. As always, talk to a tax specialist for professional advice. *Lesson: Be careful about buying options with your retirement money.*

13. Sam constantly had too much money at risk on individual trades. Therefore, he crossed the line from trading to gambling. He exhibited all the symptoms of a gambler, and sadly, Sam didn't realize it, even after he had lost a big chunk of his retirement account. When relying on Lady Luck to help you make money, you may as well bet on red or black at a casino. Sometimes you don't realize you have crossed over to the wild side. *Lesson: Don't become a gambler, and if you recognize that you have done so, stop trading.*

14. It was risky for Sam to buy calls before an earnings announcement, and to buy when prices were high. Instead, he bet too much, got overwhelmed with too many positions, and lost money. *Lesson: Keep it simple.*

15. Sam kept beating himself up for not taking a profit when he had the chance. This caused him emotional stress and affected the way he traded all week. He was also trying to get

even and seek revenge on the stocks that cost him money. Instead of trading like a scientist, he acted like Chicken Little. To be a winning trader, you must keep unhealthy emotions under control, and if you can't, don't trade that day. *Lesson: Trade like a scientist, and never try to get even.*

16. Although adding to winning positions is acceptable at times, it must be done early, and at the right time. (Yes, timing is everything. We will discuss how to get the timing right later.) With options, it's easy to add so late that you end up chasing, which usually ends poorly. And if you do add to a winner, do not invest more than you can afford to lose. *Lesson: Add to winners early, if possible, and with few contracts (and if late, don't trade at all).*

17. Sam had no clue about market or stock trends and didn't look at a chart or try to learn basic technical analysis, which might have helped him find better entries and exits. As it turned out, he just entered and exited positions on a whim rather than based on a plan, strategy, or a chart. *Lesson: Learn basic technical analysis before trading.*

18. Sam had profits within an hour, but he made no attempt to protect those profits. He should have either sold the options for a decent profit or sold when the profits started to disappear. The ability to sell winning options for a profit, or sell losers when they are still manageable, is the key to successful trading, although this is not easy. In fact, you could spend your entire trading career trying to master these two tasks. When to protect profits and when to sell winners is the challenge that every trader faces, especially when the market constantly fluctuates during the day. Sam never considered these difficulties when he strolled into the options market without a clue about what he was doing. *Lesson: There is a lot more to trading options than most people realize.*

19. Although no one expects traders to sit in front of a computer all day, it's also not wise to leave in the middle of a complex trade while holding high-risk positions. Sam left a large open option position, and unfortunately, it went against him within minutes. Many unlucky traders lose large sums of money by leaving their computer for lunch or snacks. Perhaps wait until the position is resolved before taking a break, or eat lunch at your trading desk. By the way, do not trade or hold open positions when you are on vacation. *Lesson: Keep your eyes on your option positions at all times.*

20. Puts are not easy to manage, but Sam didn't know that because he had zero real-life experience and zero training. Just reading a few books on options didn't provide him enough knowledge. He was woefully unprepared to enter the options market and trade, and it cost him dearly. If he had been properly educated, he would have been cautious when buying puts, would not have held them for long, and would have taken the profits when offered. Sam just wasn't ready to trade with real money. *Lesson: Get an options education before trading options.*

21. Although following too many technical indicators is a mistake, not using any is also a mistake. Sam should have had at least one or two indicators on his charting software, or he should have learned the strategies in this book. With no plan, no strategy, and no indicators, Sam was doomed to fail. *Lesson: Study market indicators or charts.*

22. Each day, Sam should have kept records of any mistakes that he knew he had made. He should have taken the time to reflect on why he had lost money. One example is why his winning position turned to a loser. He didn't understand or evaluate his mistakes, so he repeated them. *Lessons: Write down your trading mistakes. Determine why you lost money.*

23. Sam didn't understand how the options market worked,
     and perhaps assumed it was logical. If you want logic, play
     chess. So Sam waltzed into the options market with a lot of
     money and no idea what he was doing. Not surprisingly, he
     lost money. It was not the fault of the options market, but
     the fact that Sam was unprepared and uneducated. *Lesson:
     Educate yourself before beginning to trade (one of the rea-
     sons you are reading this book!).*

24. Sam was so new to trading that he also didn't develop a daily
     routine. In addition, he lost control of his emotions, and then
     his account. He bought high-flying stocks that moved with-
     out a clear reason for the purchase. He also bought stocks
     at random without taking the time to study their personal-
     ities and how they traded at different times during the day.
     Lesson: Have a plan and strategy before buying or selling.

25. The Apple earnings report was a two-edged sword. Although
     everyone had predicted the earnings report would be pos-
     itive (it was), no one predicted that guidance (expectations
     for the future) would be negative, or how the market would
     react. It was too risky for Sam to hold a one-sided (bullish)
     stance before an earnings report. Perhaps his bullish view
     was understandable, but his investment was way too large.
     Making a big options bet before an earnings announcement
     is guessing, not trading. The other problem was that Sam was
     so certain he was right and bet accordingly. Unfortunately,
     the stock market is not a fairy godmother and does not
     comply with your wishes. *Lesson: Be cautious about buying
     options before a major earnings announcement.*

26. Often, one bad trade leads to another, and that's what hap-
     pened to Sam. To avoid this mistake, recognize a bad trade
     when you make one. Then exit the position and ignore all
     thoughts of earning back your money. It is no longer your
     money. It belongs to someone else. Whenever you recog-

nize a trading mistake, and always when you make a second one, stop trading. Collect your thoughts and consider starting over with a clear mind by selling all positions. *Lesson: Stop trading if you are losing money.*

27.   Another mistake that Sam made was that when he saw that his stocks were spiking up or down, he chased after them. Chasing is not trading. If Sam had read this book, or had more experience, he would have known that stocks that gap higher or lower at the open often stall and reverse. *Lesson: Don't chase spiking stocks. (Or if using technical analysis, don't get trapped in a gap.)*

28.   When Sam bought Tesla, he was buying a volatile stock (at least it was volatile at the time he bought it). Hot stocks like this can cost money if you are on the wrong side. Because Tesla was so unpredictable and volatile, even one contract was too risky, and too expensive. If Sam had bought more contracts, one wrong move could have destroyed his account. The general rule is that the more volatile and wild the stock, the less money you can afford to commit to the trade. *Lesson: Avoid trading unpredictable and volatile stocks, or trade small.*

29.   One of the most important rules of trading is to sell losers quickly. It's drilled into every trader's head. Sam knew this rule, but for some reason, he didn't follow it. This is a common problem for traders who lack discipline. They simply refuse to accept the loss and won't exit. Discipline requires knowing your own rules and then following them. Once the loss reached the maximum that he had established (or should have established) for the trade, he should have sold. When the trade losses were small, they were acceptable. In addition, when his winner turned to a loser, that was a flashing warning sign. *Lesson: Cut losses when they reach the limit you have established prior to making the trade.*

30. Sam traded options without understanding how implied volatility affects options prices. He overpaid for the options because implied volatility was high. Although Sam thought he knew how to trade options, he lacked basic knowledge of options pricing. It was unwise of Sam to trade options until he had gained more experience. *Lesson: Understand basic option concepts including implied volatility before trading.*

31. Another huge mistake that Sam made was doubling down on a losing position. His SPY puts were already bleeding money, but because his neighbor egged him on, Sam added money to a loser. He even knew it was a mistake, but he couldn't help himself. It was a mixture of greed and hope that caused him to make this mistake. *Lesson: Only losers add to losers.*

32. A clue that Sam was in over his head was his apparent physical reactions. When he felt sick and dizzy and afraid about the positions he held, that was an unmistakable clue that he was holding too many positions. His inability to sleep was another clue. He should have reduced his holdings down to the sleeping point, or listened to his body. *Lesson: Pay attention to your physical reactions.*

33. Another error that Sam made was a failure to diversify. He used his entire retirement account for trading options, a fatal error. He should have separated his retirement account from the options account. Sam could have taken a small amount, perhaps 10 percent, and used that for trading. Knowing how much can be at risk in the options market is a mandatory skill. Others with less money should also limit how much to trade. *Lessons: Don't use your retirement account to trade options, and don't trade with money that you can't afford to lose.*

Trading Scared

Sam didn't have this problem, but it's essential that you not rely on the options market to pay off your bills or debt. Although in theory it sounds wonderful to use the options (or stock) market to pay off your credit cards, in reality, the plan may backfire.

First, by using the options market as an ATM machine, you are at risk of "trading scared," which results in making mistakes. In a worst-case scenario, you could lose your trading money and still have substantial debts.

My first suggestion is to keep your trading account separate from other investments. If you can generate substantial profits from trading options, you should periodically move money out of the trading account into less risky investments.

But if your goal is to make so much money from trading options that you can solve all your financial problems, the chances are that you will take on too much risk. The pressure to continuously make money could be too great, resulting in mistakes, and more lost money.

Finally, because Sam was a beginner with substantial assets, he should have started trading with much less trading capital. Also, just because he was allowed to trade options in his IRA didn't mean he should have.

· · · · · · · ·

Hopefully, you have learned a few lessons from Sam's devastating experience. Please don't think that any of the above can't happen to you, because anyone who does not respect risk is liable to make some of these mistakes.

As I said at the beginning of this chapter, you should review these lessons on occasion. Even more important, maintain a list of the most common mistakes that you make and the lessons learned.

Bottom line: If people tell you it's easy to find success when trading options, or stocks, don't believe them. It's not. Although it's fun to make money, never forget how painful losses can be, which is the reason you must understand and manage risk.

· · · · · · · ·

Now that you know about the potential risks of trading options, as well as what happens when you aren't disciplined, it's time to learn how to make money using a variety of options strategies, some that are very different. Take a deep breath because the next part may be a new experience for you.

PART TWO

THE TEST TRADING STRATEGY

Now that you have a better idea of the potential risks of trading options, it's time to get to work. In this part, you will be introduced to the Test Trading Strategy, a new way of identifying winning stocks.

Because so many new ideas are introduced in Part Two, it may take some time to understand the material and feel confident about using it. I did my best to lay out all the information using a conversational tone and an easy-to-read format.

There is no need to rush through this strategy. At times, you may have to read some sections more than once. Most importantly, try to keep an open mind as you are introduced to a number of simple methods that you have never heard of before. I can promise you this: The information you will learn in this part will be unlike anything you have read anywhere else.

3

The Test Trading Account

In this chapter, you will learn how to set up a *test trading account* (also known as a simulated trading or paper money program) at your brokerage or on the internet. Many brokerage firms have spent time and money developing paper money accounts, which I believe are one of the most useful and unappreciated tools ever created.

Many traders have used simulated trading programs to test their strategies or ideas or to backtest (evaluate how a strategy would have worked in the past). In the trading community, many traders aren't fans of using simulated programs because they believe the programs are unrealistic and unhelpful. I could not disagree more.

In fact, I made the following discovery: Almost every day, you can use a test trading account to find a winning stock or index to trade. Don't believe anyone who says simulated trading isn't useful.

Unfortunately, I once thought that also, but I was wrong. In fact, one of the best ways to learn how to trade, earn profits, and avoid losing money is through a virtual trading account. I wish I had known that when I first started trading!

As mentioned earlier, you will learn how to use a test trading account to find winning stocks. It's easy to set up and implement, and it should help you find potential winners nearly every day.

Suggestions

- Find out if your brokerage firm has a simulated or paper money account so customers can test before they trade. If your firm doesn't, it should. I spoke with several brokerage firms as I wrote this book. The representatives told me that their firms were developing simulated trading accounts (or thinking about it). Let's hope that in the future every broker has a test trading account available for its clients.

- If you are unable to access a simulated trading program, don't worry. I give instructions for how to use the Test Trading Strategy even when you can't paper-trade. Part of what you'll need to do involves keeping manual records. See the sidebar, "If You Don't Have a Paper Trading Account" which you'll find at the end of the chapter.

- After reading about the Test Trading Strategy, if you are more comfortable using traditional methods such as technical analysis, feel free to do so. You can use both methods, and in fact, I recommend it.

Introducing the Test Trading Strategy

When I was a teacher, I learned that the success of my lessons depended on how well I prepared each day before class. The better my preparation and planning, the higher the chances that the lesson would succeed.

It's the same when trading in the options market. In fact, your success or failure as a trader usually begins before the market opens at 9:30 a.m. ET. If you don't prepare properly before the market opens, your chance of success is greatly reduced.

Most traders, especially beginners, don't know how to prepare for the trading day. I'm going to change that right now by introducing you to the Test Trading Strategy. If you have the patience to set it up and use it properly, I believe it will dramatically improve your trading results. It did for me.

With the Test Trading Strategy, you will use a test trading account to find winning stocks and exchange-traded funds (ETFs). Another benefit of using this strategy is that it helps you determine when to trade, or when to avoid trading because market conditions are too dangerous.

The Theory Behind the Test Trading Strategy

I'll tell you a story that should help explain more about the Test Trading Strategy. Imagine that you go to the racetrack and decide to place a bet on a horse. As you may know, before the race begins, you can place a wager on one or more horses that you believe will do well (win, place, or show). You'll make money on your bet if the horse you choose finishes in the top three.

Most importantly, once the bell rings and the race begins, you are prohibited from placing any bets. Imagine if that rule were changed so that soon after the starting bell, while the race was in progress, you could place a bet on a horse. If allowed, you'd obviously place your bet on the one or two horses in the lead.

With the Test Trading Strategy, every day you attempt to identify the one or two stocks or indexes that are going to be in the lead after the market opens. Once you have identified potential winning stocks, you will place your bets with options (or buy the stock if you are an investor).

Put another way, although at the racetrack you are not allowed to place a bet on horses that are already in the lead, in the stock market you are allowed to buy options on stocks that are in the lead and making money. These are the true winners, that is, stocks that not only trade higher after the market opens, but continue to trade higher most of the day (or longer).

Although you can make the most money during a bull market, at other times there are often one or two stocks that are the most profitable (you will learn how to identify them later). Your job is to find the strongest stocks that are steadily rising all day. On the days when no stock is in the lead, you will not trade at all.

Some of you may recognize this strategy being similar to "following the trend," and there are similarities. It's true that you can make money when you catch an uptrend and buy calls (or buy puts in a downtrend).

With the Test Trading Strategy, however, you do not simply buy based on the direction of a trend on a chart. In fact, the traditional trend-following strategy is fraught with risks. Just like in a horse race, the underlying stock might start off strong, but soon after you buy, the stock may lose steam and reverse direction. Blindly following, or chasing, the trend will often lead to disastrous results. I'll help you avoid making that mistake.

With the Test Trading Strategy, although you do follow trends, you will not buy a stock unless it is a winner based on the criteria you set up in the test trading account. Keep reading to find the exact details on how to find these winners.

> *Bottom line:* The strategy you are about to learn is a trend-following, momentum strategy. The key to success is finding a moneymaking stock that is trending higher and then following it.

The Test Trading Strategy is primarily designed to go long stocks or indexes using *calls.* Those who are bearish on the stock market and want to buy *puts* will learn how to do that in Chapter 7.

Setting Up the Test Trading Account

First, I assume that you already have a brokerage account and that you received permission from the brokerage firm to trade options. (If not, you can apply at your convenience. In this chapter, we will not be making real trades, so you have time to call your brokerage to set up an options trading account.)

Most importantly, it's helpful if you have access to a test trading account. Most brokers allow simulated trades, but if yours does not, you can still use the strategies in this book. My guess is that every brokerage firm will eventually have a simulated or virtual trading program. Why? Customers like yourself will demand it.

At the time of this writing, the brokerages that do have paper money accounts include TD Ameritrade, Interactive Brokers, TradeStation, and E*TRADE. I am certain there will be more by the time you have read this book, and I will list their names in future editions.

One of the most powerful simulated trading accounts is the paperMoney® Virtual Stock Market Simulator on the thinkorswim® platform from TD Ameritrade. The screens are easy to use, and you're given an unlimited amount of paper money. Anyone in the world with an email address is allowed to use the program for 60 days free of charge (even if you don't have an account with the company). I strongly recommend considering this program if you adopt the Test Trading Strategy. To practice trade with a paper money account, go to this website: platform.thinkorswim.com. (Contact TD Ameritrade for further assistance.)

> *Hint:* If you have friends who want to trade options or stocks but don't have a brokerage account, suggest they start with the paper money account above.

Another alternative is to open a simulated trading game at third-party websites. One of the easiest to use is at Investopedia, which gives you $1 million in paper money. The simulated account duplicates real trades, although quotes are delayed by 15 minutes. Even with the 15-minute delay, you can use my methods to find winning stocks, and that is at the heart of the strategies you will learn in this chapter.

You can also set up a simulated trading game at MarketWatch. com, which provides $100,000 in play money and has a 15-minute quote delay.

Note: At the end of this chapter, read the sidebar, "If You Don't Have a Paper Trading Account," if you want to paper-trade but don't have access to any paper trading account.

It usually takes no more than 10 minutes to set up the practice trading account. Not everyone has the time or motivation to set it up in advance. But you will learn, as I did, that once you see the results of the Test Trading Strategy, you may never want to trade without it. That depends on how much time you want to devote to its use and whether you think it will increase your trading profits.

Once again, if you are using other methods such as technical analysis, you can combine the methods. There is no reason to choose one strategy over another. The Test Trading Strategy is simply another way of analyzing the overall market and individual stocks, but it is not the only method.

And now, let's get started!

Calls and Puts

Although there are dozens of options strategies, many that are quite complex, the only options strategy covered in this book is to buy calls and puts. No matter how complex your favorite options strategy, buying calls and puts is at its heart.

While buying options is deceptively easy to understand, making money at it has been elusive for many traders. I'm hoping I can help improve your odds of success with the Test Trading Strategy.

Step 1: Create Your Watch List

Creating a Watch List, which is simply a list of stocks, ETFs, or other securities that you are following, is essential to your success as a trader. Basic information such as stock quotes, bid-ask prices, volume, and other important details should be displayed. You can view the Watch List on an iPad, tablet, computer, or smartphone.

Add SPY and QQQ to Your Watch List

You will start by adding SPY and QQQ, but you should also be monitoring the Dow Jones Industrial Average (DJIA) and the Standard & Poor's 500 Index (SPX, or S&P 500). Later, you will add other securities to the list, including individual stocks.

I can't stress enough how important it is to have a strong Watch List. Many of the stocks in your Watch List will have a high correlation to the overall stock market, and represent the core group of stocks that you will monitor, and possibly trade each day.

The first two entries in your Watch List will be SPY and QQQ. Next, we will add individual stocks to the list. By the time you finish, you will have a very strong Watch List. Most of the trades you make will be stocks that are in this list.

Step 2: Add Individual Stocks to Your Watch List

Almost all experienced traders have a Watch List of stocks they are monitoring or considering trading, and you should, too.

Too many traders glance at the stock quotes but make little use of the data. Instead of passively watching stock quotes, you will use the list to find winning stocks when the opportunity presents itself. Remember to pay attention to how this core group of stocks behaves each day.

To add individual stocks to your Watch List, you must decide which stocks to include. Below are the criteria that I used to create my list, but you are free to make adjustments depending on your experience or needs.

If you are a relatively new trader who has never built a Watch List, use the criteria below until you feel confident that you know which stocks belong on your list. You will periodically add and remove stocks until you settle on a core group of stocks.

The Watch List should include no more than 80 to 90 stocks. If you have never built a Watch List, 80 to 90 stocks might seem excessive. Please don't worry, because you will never trade that many stocks. When you begin using the Test Trading Strategy, only a few winners will appear each day, usually no more than 5 or 10 stocks.

Criteria for Which Stocks to Include

Here are the initial criteria I suggest when building your Watch List:

1. Include underlying stocks that are at least $50 per share or higher. (Feel free to include lower-priced stocks if you want, but I prefer higher-priced stocks that make larger point moves. It's a personal choice.)
2. Include the most active and liquid stocks in the market. These stocks are widely held, including by mutual funds, indexes, banks, and hedge funds, the kind of stocks that are often mentioned in the media. These stocks include some of the most successful companies in the world. They can be volatile at times, and occasionally undergo rapid price changes. (That's good for traders who own calls or puts.)

Stocks Not to Include

Many stocks are inappropriate for a Watch List. Keep in mind that a stock on my list doesn't have to be on yours. I don't include underlying stocks that are designated as ADRs (American Depositary Receipts), representing investment in a foreign company's stock. In addition, I don't include stocks of companies that I don't recognize or that have unusual stock symbols.

Not only are these potentially risky to trade, but they are likely to be illiquid (not much trading activity). Stick with the stocks of companies you know and have heard about.

My Watch List

As an example, following are the stocks that were on my Watch List at the time that I wrote this book. These names are subject to change at any time, and no doubt the list is different on the day you are reading these pages. I make changes every few weeks or months.

In alphabetical order, the following individual stocks are included in my Watch List: A (Agilent Technologies), ABT (Abbott Laboratories), AAPL (Apple), ABBV (AbbVie), ADBE (Adobe), AMAT (Applied Materials), AMD (Advanced Micro Devices, AMGN (Amgen), AMZN (Amazon), ATVI (Activision), AXP (American Express), BA (Boeing), BABA (Alibaba Group), BBY (Best Buy), BIDU (Baidu), BMY (Bristol-Myers), BX (The Blackstone Group), BYND (Beyond Meat), C (Citigroup), CAT (Caterpillar), CL (Colgate-Palmolive), CLX (Clorox), CMG (Chipotle), COST (Costco), CRM (Salesforce), CRWD (CrowdStrike), CTXS (Citrix), CVS (CVS Health), DE (Deere), DFS (Discover), DIS (Disney), DOCU (DocuSign), EBAY (eBay), ETSY (Etsy), EXPE (Expedia), FB (Facebook), FDX (FedEx), FSLY (Fastly), GILD (Gilead Sciences), GIS (General Mills), GLD (Gold Trust), GOOG (Alphabet), GS

(Goldman Sachs), HD (Home Depot), HLT (Hilton Worldwide Holdings), HON (Honeywell International), IBM (International Business Machines), INTC (Intel), JNJ (Johnson & Johnson), JPM (JP Morgan Chase), KO (Coca-Cola), LLY (Eli Lily), LMT (Lockheed Martin), LOW (Lowe's), LULU (lululemon athletica), MA (Mastercard), MAR (Marriott International), MCD (McDonald's), MMM (3M), MRK (Merck), MSFT (Microsoft), MU (Micron), NFLX (Netflix), NKE (Nike), NVDA (Nvidia), OSTK (Overstock), PEP (PepsiCo), PG (Procter & Gamble), PYPL (PayPal Holdings), QCOM (Qualcomm), ROKU (Roku), SBUX (Starbucks), SHOP (Shopify), SPLK (Splunk), SQ (Square), TGT (Target), TSLA (Tesla), TWLO (Twilio), TXN (Texas Instruments), UPS (United Parcel Service), V (Visa), VZ (Verizon), W (Wayfair), WBA (Walgreens Boots Alliance), WMT (Walmart), WYNN (Wynn Resorts), XLNX (Xilinx), and ZM (Zoom Video Communications).

Add these stocks to your watch list, and any others that you wish. You now have a powerful Watch List. When it's time to trade, you will primarily be buying options on the stocks and ETFs from this list.

A Starting Point

Consider the list as a starting point. As economic conditions change and the years go by, so will your list of stocks change. Some stocks will decline below $40 or $50 per share or fall out of favor with institutions. New companies will emerge in the future, and you may choose to include them. Old favorites will be removed.

Figure 3.1 shows a screenshot of a partial Watch List.

Symbol ▲	Name	Last	Change	%Chg	Open	High	Low
＋ $DOWI	Dow Jones Industrials Average	27,930.33	+190.60	+0.69%	27,758.13	27,959.48	27,686.78
＋ A	Agilent Technologies	98.30	+0.52	+0.53%	97.87	98.32	97.27
＋ AAPL	Apple Inc	513.12	+15.64	+3.14%	477.05	514.18	477.00
＋ ABBV	Abbvie Inc	95.40	+0.54	+0.57%	95.20	95.40	94.32
＋ ABT	Abbott Laboratories	103.00	+0.60	+0.59%	101.63	103.00	100.84
＋ ADBE	Adobe Systems Inc	478.00	+4.78	+1.01%	477.09	479.40	470.34
＋ AMAT	Applied Materials	62.97	+0.70	+1.12%	63.10	63.28	61.92
＋ AMD	Adv Micro Devices	84.38	+0.57	+0.68%	83.29	84.47	82.23
＋ AMGN	Amgen Inc	237.38	-0.26	-0.11%	238.88	238.88	235.51
＋ AMZN	Amazon.com Inc	3,311.70	+26.98	+0.82%	3,295.00	3,314.39	3,275.39
＋ ATVI	Activision Blizzard	83.63	+0.42	+0.50%	84.05	84.09	82.73
＋ AXP	American Express Company	97.00	+0.85	+0.88%	96.49	97.65	95.96
＋ BA	Boeing Company	169.92	+2.42	+1.44%	168.35	170.08	167.27
＋ BABA	Alibaba Group Holding	273.32	+7.52	+2.83%	259.03	273.43	258.31
＋ BBY	Best Buy Company	117.00	+3.00	+2.63%	112.00	117.00	111.95
＋ BIDU	Baidu Inc	123.90	+1.45	+1.18%	121.54	123.90	121.10
＋ BMY	Bristol-Myers Squibb Company	62.50	+0.31	+0.50%	62.22	62.50	61.74
＋ IWM	Russell 2000 Ishares ETF	155.97	+1.36	+0.88%	154.48	156.00	153.60

FIGURE 3.1 Partial Watch List
Source: Barchart.com.

Step 3: Set Up the Test Trading Account

Now that you have a Watch List, you are going to set up your test trading account. It's not enough to simply have a Watch List, which is on every trader's screen. We are going to do something quite different from most traders: we are going to make paper money trades with certain stocks that fit our criteria.

If you don't know how to enter into a trade with individual stocks or options, don't panic. Step-by-step instructions for setting up the test trading account are included below. It should only take a few minutes to complete the practice trade.

If this is the first time you ever made a trade, it may take a little longer. Speed is not important right now. At first, this process may seem more complicated than it really is. Also, it's better that you make these practice trades in a paper money account than risking real money.

> *Note to novice traders:* If you are unfamiliar with option vocabulary or have never made an options trade, you can go to Chapter 10, "Options Minicourse," before proceeding. Then the following instructions will make more sense.

And now, let's learn a new strategy to help you identify and buy winning stocks.

Step 4: Place Paper Money Trades in the Test Trading Account

Remember, we are not making a real trade, but only a simulated trade, in the test trading account. Below are specific instructions on how to set up your test trading account for trading options on individual stocks.

Let's Begin!

Before the market opens, let's set up the test trading account to place orders. Instead of betting real money on any stock that moves higher right out of the starting gate, you will use data from the paper trading account to identify winning stocks. Once we find those winners, we will buy calls on stocks that have the most potential to trend higher.

Adjust the Test Trading Parameters

Before you make test trades with individual stocks, you should adjust the test trading account parameters. Brokers typically provide a limited sum of paper money to use for purchases.

Change that amount so that you have at least $100,000 and up to $5 million in the paper money account. You are using that figure so you can use paper money to buy dozens of stocks without being limited. The more paper money you are allowed to use, the better. If your simulated trading program limits how much paper money you can use (some simulated programs have $100,000 limits), it's not a problem. You can work with smaller limits by lowering the number of shares and contracts you purchase. Although we are placing an order to buy 100 shares of stock in the test trading account, feel free to buy fewer shares.

> *Hint:* Every night, you should clear out (reset) all the day's trades and start over. At the start of each day, you want to have zero positions in your test trading account. To reset the day's trades and change preferences (such as increasing the amount of paper money), you must download the program to a computer. If you're unable to change preferences, contact the brokerage firm for help.

Let's continue building our test trading account by making test trades of individual stocks that fit our criteria. This is going to take only a few minutes each day. If you are a beginner, the following instructions may seem confusing at first, but after a few days of making entries, it will be easier to understand. As I said before, the more you practice, the sooner you will learn how to trade.

Thirty Minutes Before the Market Opens

At least 30 minutes before the market opens, take the following steps.

Step 5: Check Stock Quotes in the Watch List

Begin by looking at the stock quotes in your Watch List as well as the major indexes. Even before the market opens, you will get an idea how the stock market will open by looking at the quotes in the futures market. As I like to say, the futures tell the future.

Step 6: Identify Any Stock That Has Moved Up 1 Point or 1 Percent

The key to making money using the Test Trading Strategy (or almost any strategy) starts before the market opens. Don't forget your main mission: You are on the hunt for stocks that are potential winners. There are numerous ways to find these winners, and I'll show you my favorite.

Before we begin, I want you to understand that the criteria that I use are flexible. That means that although I'll tell you the parameters that I use, feel free to make adjustments as you see fit. There is no best answer as long as you are able to identify winners.

Start by scanning through your list of active stocks in your Watch List on the brokerage screen. The criteria I use are as follows, and they're very simple.

You are looking for any stock in your Watch List that has moved up by more than 1 point (or by 1 percent) in the premarket. Some traders prefer to look at percentage moves rather than price changes measured in dollars.

The Test Trading Strategy was designed to be flexible. Consider the 1 point or 1 percent moves as guidelines, not rules. For those who prefer to trade lower-priced stocks, focus more on percentage moves than point moves.

No matter whether you use points or percentages, focus on finding winning stocks that are on the move higher and buy them in the test trading account. And if the stocks you chose keep moving higher, consider making a real trade (details on making a real trade come later).

If you choose stocks that have made large percentage moves in the premarket, I suggest that you not choose stocks that have spiked higher than 8 or 9 percent. The reason is that stocks that spike too high and too fast at the open tend to reverse direction quickly, and so are too risky to trade.

Points or Percentages

Everyone has a different idea concerning which stocks to buy. Just because I have been writing about trading higher-priced stocks doesn't mean that you should do so.

I also know that a 1-point move on a $50 stock is effectively 10 times greater than the same 1-point move on a $500 stock. That is why many of you will look at percentage moves, not point moves. Whether you use points or percentages, don't forget the number one goal: Find winning stocks.

I hope that you will be encouraged to experiment to see which approach works best for you and the stocks that you trade. In the premarket, look for stocks that have the most potential. At first, use the 1 point or 1 percent criteria. With experience and training, you will learn to quickly scan through the Watch List and find stocks that are potential winners.

In the next chapter, you will learn what to do with these winners. For now, take your time and find stocks in the premarket that are ready to rise at the market open.

On some days, especially when the market is falling, there may only be a few stocks that fit the criteria. On other days, when the market is ready to rocket higher at the open, many of the stocks on your list will be up by more than 1 point (or 1 percent). From this group, profitable stocks will emerge.

Power of the Probe

Once you've identified potential winners, it's time to probe. By probing before using real money, you identify true winners that can make it all the way to the finish line. I'd rather probe with paper money than risk losing real money.

From the test trading account, do the following.

Step 7: In the Test Trading Account, Place an Order to Buy 100 Shares of Each Stock That Is at Least 1 Point (or 1 Percent) Higher

After finding stocks that fit our criteria, place a market order to buy 100 (or more) shares of stock in the premarket.

You might wonder why we are buying shares of stock and not options. The reason is that the options markets do not open until 9:30 a.m. ET. Because we are unable to trade options until the regular market opens, we buy stocks in the premarket.

The market order you placed to buy stock in the premarket will be filled in the practice account once the stock begins trading, and that is 9:30 a.m. or later. The paper money purchases we are making in the premarket will lead us to the winning stocks.

> *Note:* Although we are placing an order to buy 100 shares in the test trading account, feel free to buy fewer shares if your brokerage limits the amount of money you may use. The Test Trading Strategy was designed to be flexible, so use the number of shares that makes sense to your trading style.

Based on my research, I found that entering orders to buy 100 shares is the appropriate number for most stocks. However, you can also buy more shares. Also, you may use fewer shares when buying high-priced stocks (over $1,000 per share), which will make more sense after the market opens and you can see the results on your position page.

Typically, you will buy 100 shares of no more than 20 or 30 stocks. Making these paper trade purchases in the premarket usually takes less than 10 minutes, but you may tighten the parameters; for example, only include stocks that have moved up by 2 points (or by a certain percentage).

> *Note:* Although this book is aimed at options traders, as a bonus, if you trade stocks, you can use the same information described in this section to buy winning stocks as well as options.

> *Important:* Be sure you are in the test trading program before making these trades!

Example Orders

Here are two examples of which orders to place in the test trading account before the market opens:

Example #1: Place an Order to Buy 100 Shares of Apple in the Test Trading Account

Starting in alphabetical order at the top of your Watch List (Figure 3.1), you see that the price of A (Agilent Technologies) is $.52 (or .53%) higher in the premarket. Because it does not meet the $1 (or 1 percent) requirement, do not make a paper money purchase. Skip this stock for today.

Next on your list is AAPL (Apple), which is higher by $15.64 (or 3.14%) in the premarket. Here is the important part: Make a paper money order to buy 100 shares of Apple *at the market.* You will buy this test stock using a *market order* (normally you would only buy with a *limit order,* but this is a test trading account). You want this order filled quickly so you can study the stock position.

Next on your list is ADBE (Adobe), which is $4.78 (or 1.01%) higher in the premarket. Enter a paper money order to buy 100 shares of Adobe *at the market.*

Scan through the list and buy 100 shares of any stock higher than 1 point (or 1 percent). Because the major indexes are higher, there will be a lot of suitable stocks. (*Reminder: If your paper trade program limits how many shares you can buy, reduce the number of shares.*)

Since this is a test trading program, we are making out-of-the-ordinary trades to help us find winning option positions and stocks.

Example #2: Place an Order to Buy 100 Shares of Boeing in the Test Trading Account

With the Test Trading Strategy, ignore any stock that is in negative territory. Therefore, on the days when the market is headed lower, you may only find a few stocks moving higher by over 1 point (or 1 percent).

Next on the list is Boeing, which is ahead by 2.42 points (or 1.44 percent) in the premarket. Since Boeing should open higher, make a paper money order to buy 100 shares of Boeing at the market.

> *Note:* Don't consider these hard-and-fast rules, but these are the criteria that worked from testing and experimenting. As you gain more knowledge, you can make adjustments.

Keep scanning through the stocks in your Watch List. Each time you see a stock that is up by more than 1 point or 1 percent in the premarket, make a paper money order to buy 100 shares. Again, do not make a real purchase. We are making these paper money purchases to help us find winning stocks in the future. It will make sense later as you keep reading.

On some days, when the premarket is extremely bullish, it's possible that a larger number of stocks on the Watch List will be up by more than 1 point or 1 percent. If there are too many stocks for you to comfortably study, then change the criteria for that day so that only the biggest movers are added. For example, you could change the criterion for percentage from 1 percent to 2 percent. Even better, you could only choose stocks that are up by both 1 point and 1 percent. That will trim the number of stocks that are in play.

On other days, perhaps all the major indexes are going to plunge at the open based on the premarket prices. When you scan the stocks in your Watch List, you may see that nearly every stock is down by 1 or 2 points in the premarket.

When this occurs, you will not add stocks that are falling. If there are any stocks that are up in the premarket (by any amount), and there could be only a few, you can add them. Keep in mind that if the overall market is headed lower, it could be risky to go long with most individual stocks.

Add Other Stocks to the Test Trading Account

In addition to test buying stocks on the Watch List that fit your criteria, you can also look for other stock candidates (if you have time). For example, you might want to scan financial websites that list stocks that are moving up by more than 1 point in the premarket.

Perhaps there is breaking good news on the stock, or an analyst made a buy recommendation, or the stock in a company beat earnings. Don't be concerned with *why* a stock is moving up in the premarket. All that matters is that it fits your criteria for a test purchase.

To find stocks that are moving higher by 1 point (or 1 percent) in the premarket, go to websites such as MarketWatch, CNN Money, Yahoo Finance, and Market Chameleon, to name a few. These websites have links to stocks that are the most active in the premarket. Obviously, there are other websites that show the same information, but these are the top four that I monitor.

It is your choice whether to buy shares of the "guest" stocks above. Typically, they are "one-day wonders," and often rise and then flame out within the same day. When there is not enough time to add guest stocks to the list, concentrate on the original list of stocks in your Watch List.

Other Ways to Find Winning Stocks

Before we discuss how to implement the Test Trading Strategy, be aware that there are still other ways to find potential winners. If you prefer, you can choose one or both of the following methods.

1. Use technical analysis and buy a stock or index when it moves above its moving average. This is one of the most popular methods to find winning stocks. Moving averages are simple and easy to use, and are described in Chapter 11.
2. Use intraday technical indicators such as VWAP (volume weighted average price) or the NYSE Tick to help you decide when to buy. These indicators are beyond the scope of this book but can be learned from other sources (such as on the internet). In addition, many day traders rely on MACD (Moving Average Convergence Divergence) to help with buy and sell decisions.

Be Picky About the Stocks You Buy

Just because a stock on your Watch List is up by over 1 point (or 1 percent) doesn't mean you should buy it in the test trading account. There are several times when you should not waste your time making even a paper money trade. For example, if you notice that the underlying stock is spiking higher by over 8 or 9 percent in the pre-market, don't buy it. In fact, any underlying stock that spikes higher at the open could reverse direction soon after the open. That is just too risky.

Your Daily Ritual

If using the Test Trading Strategy, your daily ritual consists of scanning the Watch List for underlying stocks that fit the 1 point (or 1 percent) criteria and placing an order to buy 100 shares of each. An extra benefit of repeatedly making test trades in the paper trading account is that it will help improve your trading skills. Be sure to use the test trading account to place these orders.

If You Don't Have a Paper Trading Account

Not every brokerage firm has a simulated or paper trading account. That's unfortunate because it is one of the most useful ways to identify winning stocks as well as to initiate practice trades.

  If you don't have access to a paper trading account, you can still use the Test Trading Strategy to find winning stocks. Your next choice is to use the paperMoney® Virtual Stock Market Simulator on the thinkorswim® platform from TD Ameritrade.

To practice trade with a paper money account, go to this website: platform.thinkorswim.com.

Another choice is to use Investopedia's online simulator with a 15-minute quote delay. If that doesn't meet your needs, you can also track the winners manually. Instructions are below.

The following instructions are for those without access to a paper trading account.

1. You already set up a Watch List with a list of 80 to 90 stocks. Now, during the premarket, scan through the list of stocks from your Watch List to find potential winners. Write down the name of any stock that has moved up by more than 1 point (or 1 percent). These are your target stocks.

2. Create a second Watch List and add those 1-point-higher stocks (or manually track them). These are the stocks you will be watching once the market opens. The list should include no more than 10 to 15 stocks. If too many stocks are higher by 1 point before the open, consider raising the criteria to generate a smaller list.

3. Be prepared to trade when the stock market opens at 9:30 a.m. ET.

4. Study your second Watch List and identify any stock that is continuing to move much higher. These stocks can be identified by looking at price changes or looking at the stock on a chart.

5. If you know how to use moving averages, look for stocks that are in an uptrend and breaking above their moving averages. (Moving averages and other technical indicators are explained in Chapter 11.) Feel free to use other technical indicators to help you identify strong stocks that are in an uptrend and breaking out.

6. Focus on the stocks that are steadily moving higher. Most winners appear within the first few minutes after the market opens. Ignore stocks that have faltered.

7. Keep in mind that the list of winning stocks (the true winners) that are gaining strength should be small, no more than a couple of stocks.

8. Look at the overall market environment. If the indexes are in an uptrend, the odds of success are better for stocks.

9. If you cannot find a winning stock within the first hour or so, you can stop trading individual stocks that day.

10. The key to success is being able to identify the strongest stocks that emerge from the crowd. Once you identify these winners (using technical analysis or watching the stocks on a chart), I suggest tracking their progress, but not making real trades yet. In fact, I suggest repeating this exercise for days, or weeks, until you can consistently find winning stocks. If you can identify these winners consistently, then you may be ready for the next step.

11. After you have practiced identifying winning stocks, the kind of stocks that move higher all day, then you can consider buying one call option as a probe.

12. If the one-call probe is successful, consider buying a second contract. This second probe is an optional trade. If you are new to trading, don't add to the winner. Simply monitor to see if the position is making a profit. If it is, your next task is to manage the position (for example, sell for a profit before the end of the day, if possible).

If you have time during the premarket, add "guest" stocks to your Watch List. The additions are stocks that are 1 or more points higher in the premarket. There are websites that list stocks that are the most active in the premarket. Websites with that information include MarketWatch, CNN Money, Yahoo Finance, and Market Chameleon, to name a few.

That concludes the introduction to the Test Trading Strategy. If you still don't understand how it works, don't worry, because in Chapter 9, I answer a number of questions about the strategy that should clear up any confusion.

Meanwhile, keep reading to learn how to identify winning stocks, which is the key to making money when trading options.

4

Identify True Winners

In this chapter, you will learn to identify winning stocks, that is, stocks that move higher all morning and beyond. You have already added the underlying stocks that have moved up by more than a point (or 1 percent) in the test trading account. At first, it seems to be a lot of effort to add a dozen or so stocks every day. But now your hard work will be rewarded.

You will start by using information from the test trading account to separate the wheat from the chaff, that is, to find true winners. It's not enough to buy any stock that's moving higher. That's what many inexperienced traders do.

Many novice traders purchase stocks that are zooming higher in the premarket or at the open. What they don't realize is that many of these wonder stocks stall and then reverse direction soon after the open. Many stocks start off strongly, just like in a horse race, but only a few make it to the winner's circle.

Therefore, chasing AOS (any old stock) that moves higher is a risky but popular strategy. There is nothing wrong with following a strong stock that keeps moving higher, which is what trend traders do. But chasing after any high-flying stock is too dangerous.

The first step is choosing the right underlying stock. Picking the right stock is the key to your success as a trader, but it's only the beginning. If you're wondering how you can find these profitable stocks, please be patient, because you will learn shortly.

Could Have, Would Have, Should Have

One of the hardest parts of using the Test Trading Strategy is that you will see how much money you "could" have made if you had traded with real money. That's true, but you also could have lost money. Don't fret about the stocks that got away. For now, concentrate on your education, which is more important than how much money you could have made.

And now, let's do the fun part: finding winning stocks.

Step by Step: Find Winning Stocks

You already set up a test trading account. At least 30 minutes before the market opens, you scanned through your Watch List and entered orders to purchase 100 shares (or more) of any stock that had moved by more than 1 point (or 1 percent).

The Starting Bell Rings

After the starting bell rings at 9:30 a.m. ET, watch how the dozen or so stock positions you just bought react. Right now, you are watching, not buying. Amateur traders who lack a plan tend to buy anything that moves. You, on the other hand, will be patient.

Keep in mind that it's not enough for the stocks to move higher at the open. The true winners start off strong and keep going higher all morning, and perhaps all day.

Meanwhile, there is much more to learn before you are ready to make a real trade.

Hint: There is often a lag between the starting bell when the market opens and the opening of the options market. Never start trading options until the bid-ask quotes are visible on your screen. That may be immediately, or not.

A few minutes after the stock market opens, the test trading screen will come to life. Figure 4.1 shows a screenshot of the position page soon after the market opened at 9:30 a.m. ET and after the stock orders were filled.

	SYMBOL	DESCRIPTION	QTY	PURCHASE PRICE	CURRENT PRICE	TOTAL VALUE	TODAY'S CHANGE	TOTAL GAIN/LOSS
Sell	AMD	ADVANCED MICRO DEVICES, INC.	500	$83.34	$83.34	$41,670.00	$0.00(0.00 %)	$0.00(0.00 %)
Sell	SQ	SQUARE, INC. CLASS A	500	$156.08	$156.08	$78,040.00	$0.00(0.00 %)	$0.00(0.00 %)
Sell	AAPL	APPLE INC.	500	$477.05	$480.46	$240,230.00	$1,705.00(0.71 %)	$1,705.00(0.71 %)
Sell	BABA	ALIBABA GROUP HOLDING LTD. SPONSORED ADR	500	$259.03	$258.48	$129,240.00	- $275.00(-0.21 %)	- $275.00(-0.21 %)
Sell	DE	DEERE & COMPANY	500	$196.76	$199.56	$99,777.50	$1,397.50(1.42 %)	$1,397.50(1.42 %)
Sell	SPLK	SPLUNK INC.	500	$202.50	$202.66	$101,330.00	$80.00(0.08 %)	$80.00(0.08 %)
Sell	TSLA	TESLA INC	100	$2,044.76	$2,079.48	$207,948.00	$3,472.00(1.70 %)	$3,472.00(1.70 %)
Sell	KEYS	KEYSIGHT TECHNOLOGIES INC	500	$105.62	$101.62	$50,810.00	- $2,000.00(-3.79 %)	- $2,000.00(-3.79 %)
					Total	$949,045.50	$4,379.50(0.46 %)	$4,379.50 (0.46 %)

STOCK PORTFOLIO — Trade Stock | Symbol Lookup | How-To Guide

FIGURE 4.1 Position page after market open
Source: Investopedia (www.investopedia.com/simulator)

All the stocks listed above were higher by more than 1 point (or 1 percent) in the premarket. Although the Dow and S&P 500 were flat five minutes after the opening bell, Apple, Tesla, and Deere were profitable right at the start and required close tracking. The expectation is that at least one of these three stocks will turn into a true winner.

Hint: Stocks that are big losers are ignored. Focus only on the potential winners.

1. Track the Dow (or SPX)

After the market opens, glance at the overall market indexes such as the Dow Jones Industrial Average (DJIA) or the S&P 500 (SPX).

Write down and track how much these indexes are moving up or down.

For example, you can write on a piece of paper how the Dow is performing, such as +120 and then +126, +127, +115, +130, etc. Writing down the numbers is important for future reference and to give you an idea of the direction of the Dow. You can use that information to devise a plan depending on the stock market direction.

> *Hint:* I created "trading scripts" that I study when the market opens. One script is for a higher opening, one is for a lower opening, and one is for a flat opening. I write step-by-step notes to myself exactly what to do during the trading day.

2. Search for Winners

As your paper stock orders are getting filled, you have a very important job: Search for winning stocks in the test trading account. This is the key to making money. How do you know which stocks are winners? Let's find out.

Any stock in the test trading account that is trading higher than its opening price should be watched. Obviously, you should establish your own price and profit targets, but for me, a $200 to $300 paper profit on a 100-share purchase causes me to pay close attention.

Stocks that are already up by $200 to $300 or more at the open (as seen on your trading screen) could be even bigger winners that day. You will soon learn that you don't always have to buy low to make money trading options (or stocks). You can follow the trend.

Of course, not every stock that moves higher after the open will be profitable. That is why you are going to weed out the ones that falter. Although many of the stocks you track right after the open will keep moving higher, not all of them will. In fact, most will not move much higher.

Important: Once you identify stocks that are gaining strength, and the pretend profits are increasing, write their names on a "target list." These stocks are potential winners.

The most successful stocks will become apparent soon after the opening bell. If you cannot find a profitable candidate within the first hour, you may decide to stop trading individual stocks for the rest of the day. Others may have different ideas, but generally, the Test Trading Strategy works best within the first hour or so, and after that, you may want to use other strategies.

You can use other methods such as technical analysis to select stocks. These methods are discussed in Chapter 11. This is a choice, not a rule.

Most of the time, the overall market influences stock direction. However, stocks can move higher regardless of how the market is doing. In Chapter 6, you will learn how to evaluate the overall market environment to help make trading decisions.

Your goal is to whittle down the number of stocks to no more than one or two that are likely to be true winners, the ones you want to buy in the real trading account.

3. Buy Five Calls of Any Winning Option Position in the Test Trading Account

As you can see by looking at the virtual stock positions, not all of them remained winners. Traders who buy stocks (or options) at the open take extra risk, and that's exactly what too many traders do. They chase after any stock that rallies. You aren't going to make that mistake. You will be more selective. In fact, your job is to find the true winners and avoid the one-minute wonders.

Sometimes there are only a couple of big winners, but on other days there are as many as six or seven. Focus only on ones that are the most promising. Keep scanning through the stock positions, because profits and losses change rapidly.

Do: In the test account, buy five in-the-money calls on any stock position that shows a profit in the test trading account of at least $200 or more (feel free to adjust the amount). This is the five-call probe. You are probing the early winners to see which stocks (and option positions) are continuing to move higher.

You may wonder why the first paper money purchase is an in-the-money call. This will make sense when you actually make the purchases and see the positions in the test trading account. When making real trades, we usually buy at-the-money options.

> *Hint:* There is no rule that says you have to buy 5 in-the-money calls for your initial purchase. Feel free to change the number to 10 in-the-money calls. I have experimented with both. I have found that on strong days, buying 5 calls works very well. Still, the more tests you conduct to see what works, the better.

4. Next, Buy Five More Calls of Any Winning Option Position in the Test Trading Account

If the five in-the-money calls show a profit, you will test one more time with an additional five at-the-money calls. To clarify, you have made two probes, first with five calls (in the money), and then with five more calls (at the money). The idea is to identify winning stocks that keep moving in the right direction.

If you have chosen a winner, then the five-call probe will be profitable (perhaps by $100 or $200 or more). Most importantly, if the next five-call probe is successful, and if the uptrend is verified by the one-minute chart (explained in Chapter 6), you will be ready to buy in the real brokerage account.

Some may complain that they already missed the rally. Sometimes this is true, but not always. The stocks we are interested in are the ones that rally all day. And sometimes they rally all week. I'm talking about stocks such as Apple, Amazon, and Netflix, and the list goes on, and changes every year. These are the kind of stocks we want to own with call options, and it's not only expensive stocks, either. Many lower-priced stocks also start strong and rally all day, or all week.

To repeat, you began with five in-the-money calls and followed up with five at-the-money calls. If both are profitable in the test trading account, prepare to buy calls on the winners in the real brokerage account.

Not everyone will like this trend-following strategy because you are not buying low, but instead are buying at prices that are already trending higher. In the right market environment, you can find and profit from stocks that are moving in an uptrend.

There is no specific price at which to buy the five calls. For me, if the stock position shows a profit greater than $200 to $300, I follow up with a five-call purchase. If there are multiple winning stock positions, then I may raise the bar and buy five calls on positions that are ahead by a larger sum, perhaps $400 to $500 (or choose your own amount).

Sometimes there are so many choices that it's difficult to choose which stocks to buy. Don't worry about the ones that got away. Concentrate on the ones that have the best chance of earning money.

Hint: After you've gained experience, you can skip the second probe and go directly into the real brokerage account and buy.

Watch: After you buy five additional winning calls in the test trading account, you must watch these option positions. The true winner will emerge from this list.

Other profitable positions may suddenly appear, so feel free to buy five calls on them, too (or fewer calls for high-priced stocks). I like to say that you don't find the true winners. They find you. Be on the lookout for option positions that move higher and higher, whose profits keep growing in the test trading account. That's a clue the underlying stock is rising (you can look at a chart to confirm).

Reminder: After buying five follow-up calls, if the profits keep rising, consider buying options in the real trading account. In other words, if a five-call position shows a reasonable profit, and if pretend profits are increasing, the stock could be a winner.

On some days, or even weeks, the market is boring, and stocks are languishing. When no champions appear, don't force a trade. You cannot use these methods to make money every day. Only trade when the chance of success is high and everything lines up favorably.

If you are a novice, you probably don't want to hold too many positions at one time (don't forget what happened to Sam). Instead, focus like a laser beam on only one or two positions. Then ignore all other positions in the paper trading account and manage the ones with the greatest potential.

Figure 4.2 shows what the test trading account might look like after you bought five calls.

STOCK PORTFOLIO

Trade Stock   Symbol Lookup   How-To Guide

	SYMBOL	DESCRIPTION	QTY	PURCHASE PRICE	CURRENT PRICE	TOTAL VALUE	TODAY'S CHANGE	TOTAL GAIN/LOSS
Sell	AMD	ADVANCED MICRO DEVICES, INC.	500	$83.34	$93.85	$41,925.00	$255.00(0.61 %) ↑	$255.00(0.61 %) ↑
Sell	SQ	SQUARE, INC. CLASS A	500	$156.08	$154.96	$77,477.50	-$562.50(-0.72 %) ↓	-$562.50(-0.72 %) ↓
Sell	AAPL	APPLE INC.	500	$477.05	$498.70	$249,350.00	$10,825.00(4.54 %) ↑	$10,825.00(4.54 %) ↑
Sell	BABA	ALIBABA GROUP HOLDING LTD. SPONSORED ADR	500	$259.03	$266.41	$133,205.00	$3,690.00(2.85 %) ↑	$3,690.00(2.85 %) ↑
Sell	DE	DEERE & COMPANY	500	$196.76	$201.23	$100,612.50	$2,232.50(2.27 %) ↑	$2,232.50(2.27 %) ↑
Sell	SPLK	SPLUNK INC.	500	$202.50	$202.22	$101,107.50	-$142.50(-0.14 %) ↓	-$142.50(-0.14 %) ↓
Sell	TSLA	TESLA INC	100	$2,044.76	$2,088.03	$208,803.00	$4,327.00(2.12 %) ↑	$4,327.00(2.12 %) ↑
Sell	KEYS	KEYSIGHT TECHNOLOGIES INC	500	$105.62	$96.09	$48,045.00	-$4,765.00(-9.02 %) ↓	-$4,765.00(-9.02 %) ↓
					Total	$960,525.50	$15,859.50(1.68 %) ↑	

OPTION PORTFOLIO

Trade Option   Symbol Lookup   How-To Guide

	SYMBOL	DESCRIPTION	QTY	PURCHASE PRICE	CURRENT PRICE	TOTAL VALUE	TOTAL GAIN/LOSS
Sell	AAPL2018I480	2020/09/18 2 on APPLE INC. at $480.00	10	$21.90	$34.25	$34,250.00	$12,350.00(56.39 %) ↑
Sell	AAPL2018I485	2020/09/18 2 on APPLE INC. at $485.00	5	$23.10	$31.35	$15,675.00	$4,125.00(35.71 %) ↑
Sell	SPY2018I339	2020/09/18 2 on SPDR S&P 500 ETF TRUST at $339.00	10	$5.99	$6.45	$6,450.00	$490.00(7.68 %) ↑
					Total	$56,375.00	$16,935.00(42.94 %) ↑

FIGURE 4.2   Test trading account after buying five calls
Source: Investopedia (www.investopedia.com/simulator)

In the screen in Figure 4.2, although Apple, Tesla, and Deere continued to move higher, Apple was the true winner. Once Apple was identified as a winner (because the paper money stock purchase was profitable), we bought 10 Apple calls as a probe, followed by 5 additional Apple calls as a second probe, both in the test trading account.

Since the probe was successful, we bought Apple in the real brokerage account for a substantial profit on that day. After announcing a four-to-one stock split, Apple continued to rise for several more days.

Note: I initially bought 10 calls for illustrative purposes. Usually, I start with 5 calls.

Test Trading Strategy Example

Example: Let's say you entered an order to buy 100 shares of XYZ at $79 in the premarket. After the market opens, and after you bought your shares, XYZ rallies to $82.25 per share, a 3.25-point gain. It's still moving higher. You check the 100 shares and see a $325 gain in the test trading account.

Using the strategy of adding to a winning trade, buy five XYZ in-the-money calls with a strike price of 75 in the test trading account. Monitor this position.

If XYZ keeps moving higher, the five XYZ in-the-money calls will show a profit. You will follow up by buying five XYZ at-the-money calls with a strike price at 80 in this example. In summary, start with a five-call probe; then make an additional five-call probe. This is another way of identifying stocks that are trending higher.

On some days, especially bullish days, you may be buying five calls on five to eight stocks. After making the paper money purchases, your job is to watch those winning stocks to see which ones keep going higher.

Here is the fun part: Out of this group of early winners, several stocks will move higher than the others. Zero in on any stock that keeps rising higher.

Continue scanning through the list of stocks in the test account in search of early winners. Some of the stock positions will eventually run out of gas and become losers as the stock price falls. (*Hint: Focus on the winners, not the losers.*)

It's not always easy to identify a true winner, especially when there are so many choices. Typically, the true winner will make itself known soon enough. There also may be more than one option position showing big profits, so you have to decide whether to buy only the biggest winner or buy more than one.

> *Hint:* Keep a daily record of the potential winners and how they performed. Include the stock symbol and the opening price, and jot down how much higher it opened. Include any details that will help you identify consistent winners.

In the past, stocks such as Apple, Amazon, Facebook, and many others with much lower stock prices constantly appeared on the winner's list using this strategy. When you identify these winners, you can use a variety of strategies to make money, including trading daily, trading weekly, or even buying shares of stock and holding.

Feel free to adjust any of the steps above, because they are not permanent. These steps are based on my research, but you can skip or add any steps that you believe will be helpful to do. Change the shares or contract quantities. The idea is for you to learn how to use the test trading account to find your own winners.

There are traders who won't like this profit-following strategy because it involves buying high and selling higher (we will get into selling later). In addition, they might not like getting in later than many other traders.

Unfortunately, few traders can consistently buy near the lows and sell near the highs, which is why we use trend-trading strategies. If you're a successful market timer, however, you're one of the rare ones. Trend trading is a lot less stressful and easier to use.

Summary

Although it may seem more complicated than it really is, here are the simple steps you take to use the Test Trading Strategy. Before the market opens, do the following. Remember, these are all paper money trades:

1. Enter an order to buy 100 shares (or fewer) of any stock that has risen by 1 point (or 1 percent) in the premarket.
2. Buy five calls on the stocks that are moving higher and are profitable.
3. Buy an additional five calls on the stocks that continue to move higher and are becoming more profitable.

It's really that simple. We are doing what technical analysts do, but we're looking at different data. If you actually try the strategy, you'll see how easy it is to use.

In the next chapter, you will take all the information you collected and buy calls on stocks that have made it to the winner's circle.

Optional: Buy Five Calls of SPY and QQQ

Readers who understand the Test Trading Strategy and like how it works can also buy five SPY and QQQ at-the-money calls in the test trading account as soon as the market opens.

This is not required, but speaking from experience, I can say that there is a lot to learn by watching these five call contracts in the test trading account.

Watching the five calls gives clues to market direction and sometimes warns of reversals. For example, if the market is in an uptrend but SPY and QQQ positions are not participating, and instead are reversing direction, that's a warning that the market rally may be ending. Not always, but often.

Of course, you can find the same information by looking at quotes or studying a chart, but looking at profits and losses in your paper money account provides another way to gauge market direction.

· · · · · · · ·

Now that you have identified winning stocks, and made a number of paper money trades, it's time to take all the information and buy options in the real trading account. That is what you will learn to do next.

5

Buy Options
on Winning Stocks

In this chapter, you will learn to make real trades on the stocks you have identified as winners. However, as tempting as it may be, don't make purchases with real money until you have finished and understood all of Part Two.

As you will see, on some days it's easy to find winners, especially when the market is in a strong uptrend. On other days, it's not that easy. On the slow days, either don't trade or find another strategy.

During the first half hour of the trading day, look at the option position page and try to identify winning stocks with the most potential. It's not an exact science. As mentioned earlier, many stocks will start strong and then falter.

If you are new to trading and need more time before making a real purchase, don't feel pressured. Be sure that you understand this strategy (or others) and are completely comfortable when buying options. Manage paper money positions for as long as necessary.

Now, if you are ready, let's see how to make a real purchase of the true winners.

It's Time to Trade Using the Real Brokerage Account

We're ready to make a real trade. If you are a beginner who is using this strategy for the first time, I urge you to buy only one call. As you gain experience, slowly add to your position size (two to five calls depending on the cost of each contract). Trading small means buying fewer contracts, but also putting less money at risk.

Although the odds are favorable that your stock selection will be profitable, especially if the overall market is on your side, be prepared for unexpected things to happen. There could be bad news, a bad fill, or bad luck. Until you gain the confidence that comes from earning profits using this strategy, begin with only one call at a time.

Optional: Make One More Test Trade Before Buying

If you are still not sure if you should buy, and if you are a beginner, you may make one final test trade by buying one call option that duplicates the real trade you plan to make. You may believe this is being overly cautious, and you might miss out on some highfliers, but anything you can do that minimizes risk and enhances your knowledge is a good thing.

The Five-Minute Rule

Whether you made that final test trade or not, now is the time to buy at least one call of the option of a winning stock using the *real trading account*. Before making the trade, however, use the Five-Minute Rule.

This rule reminds you to do one final check before making the actual trade. Often, when preparing to press the Enter key, traders are flush with emotion and might enter at the wrong time. To avoid mistakes, it takes less than five minutes to go through this checklist:

1. **Study the option chain.** All the information you need to make a trade is in the *option chain* including the expiration date, strike price, and bid and ask price. Before buying, be sure that all the information is correct, including the number of contracts you will enter. Many traders, anxious to buy, enter the wrong information. (For example, don't make the common beginner mistake of entering 100 call contracts when you really meant to enter only one!)

2. **Check the bid-ask spread.** Make sure the *bid-ask spread* is not too wide, and if it is, find another stock to trade. A wide bid-ask spread on an option makes it difficult to trade profitably. No one should have to fight a wide bid-ask spread when buying and then again when selling.

3. **Use a limit order.** Be sure to use a limit order, not a market order.

   Hint: You can enter a limit order between the bid and ask, or if you want a fast fill, enter a limit order at the ask price (the higher price). Negotiating for a better price rather than accepting a faster fill will make a difference in your success as a trader.

4. **Look at a chart.** Before placing a real trade, it is important to check the stock or index on a chart. In Chapter 6, you will learn how to identify behavior patterns of the overall market and individual stocks. If you are using technical analysis, don't make a trade until you study technical indicators such as moving averages, because they are often used to identify when to enter or exit.

5. **Don't be in a rush to buy.** Even if you miss one purchase, there will be another candidate tomorrow. However, if everything looks good, and the price trend is steadily moving higher (not spiking), get ready to buy for real.

6. **Track the winners.** It is important to track the winning stocks or indexes and to record their progress. That is how you will know if you are buying a true winner that is moving in a profitable direction.

Buy One Call in the Real Trading Account

If you are confident that you have found a winning stock based on the test trades, then it's time to make a real trade. Enter an order to buy one at-the-money call using a limit order and a minimum of a one-month expiration date (experienced traders may buy more contracts).

After you make the real trade, the hard work begins. If the underlying stock continues to trend higher (what you expect will happen), there should be a gain. However, if the underlying stock moves in the wrong direction, there will be a loss.

That is when you use risk management skills including a *time stop* and a *stop loss*. We will discuss these methods later in this chapter.

After You Buy One Call Option

After you have made a real options trade, there remains work to do. It's easy to buy a call after you identify a winning stock moving in an uptrend. The difficult part is knowing when to exit the position with a profit, or to sell when the underlying stock doesn't perform as expected and you are losing money on the position.

Focus on One Position at a Time

One of the biggest mistakes that options traders (as well as stock traders) make is holding too many positions at the same time. Instead of focusing on making money on one position, many try to juggle multiple positions simultaneously. That can lead to hurried decision-making and lost money. (You hopefully learned that from Sam.)

Sure, you can add a second option position, but for now, it is less risky for you to focus on only one position at a time. Don't get distracted by the ones that got away.

Monitor Your Winning Option Position

After you own at least one call, there is nothing more important than monitoring it closely. There are those who advise that you not look at profits and losses. I disagree. Look at any other information you want, but don't lose track of how much money you are making or losing. You want to be sure the option you bought has increased in value.

If you chose a winning stock at a good price, and if the overall market is moving higher, your profits should increase. Nevertheless, one breaking news story could temporarily harm profits. At the same time, do not panic or overreact if the position goes against you temporarily. With one call, losses should be manageable.

This is not the time to go to lunch or talk on the phone. Many of us have stories of losing money because we got distracted. Don't let that happen to you. After you make a purchase, focus on the position until it is sold.

When to Sell

There are two ways to manage a winning (or losing) option position.

Time Stop

A *time stop* is a useful but underutilized technique to cut losses or lock in gains. After buying an option, set a time at which you will sell the position, for either a gain or a loss. For example, after buying one call, if you have a loss after a half hour, you might consider selling. This is a decision only you can make. Most importantly, have an exit plan in place.

Keep in mind that trading options is not the same as trading stock. With stocks, you have the luxury of holding positions longer. When buying options, however, you don't have that luxury. You must be right, and quickly, or that $100 loss can turn into a $500 loss by the end of the day.

On the other hand, if you have a winning option position, you can give the option more time before selling. With a time stop, you can decide to sell before the end of the day, or perhaps hold overnight on occasion. The main point is that you decide when to sell as soon as you press the Enter key.

Stop Loss

A *stop loss* is simply an order to sell your options if the price reaches a specific limit. Most people set percentage targets or price targets. You can also set a specific sum that you are willing to lose on the position. When that loss is reached, the stop is triggered, and the option is sold. In the above example, if you buy one call, you could set a loss limit of $100 or $200 and sell when the target is reached.

Once you make a purchase and have a loss that is equal to your limit, then one of two things happens: If you entered a stop-loss order, the sale is triggered automatically. If you only have a "mental" stop loss, then it is up to you to monitor the position and sell at the appropriate time. (Note: When trading options, I prefer to use a mental stop loss.)

I can't stress how important it is to enter a stop loss as soon as you press the Enter key. Even more important, you must obey the stops. For example, let's say you bought one QQQ call contract. After pressing the Enter key, you decide that the most you will accept losing is $100 on this trade.

If the trade goes against you, and you've lost $100 or more on the trade, it's essential to sell the call. This is not the time to hope that you'll make your money back in the afternoon or the next day. Sell the position, accept the loss, and start over in the morning. It is also not the time to try to make back your money with another trade.

The main reason that most traders lose large sums of money is because they don't follow the advice above. Often, they let small losses turn into large losses by not obeying stop losses (or time stops).

Keep in mind that if you enter an automatic stop-loss order, then you do not have to worry about whether to take the loss. The stop loss will be executed without further input from the trader.

The Risks of Using the Test Trading Strategy

I hope you don't think that you have learned a "can't-lose" strategy or that there aren't risks. Like any other strategy in the financial markets, there are always risks, especially when trading options. With the Test Trading Strategy, although you can't lose more than you invested (because you are not trading on margin), you can lose 100 percent of that investment.

Here are the three main risks associated with the Test Trading Strategy:

1. You buy a winning stock that is moving higher, and it suddenly reverses direction and dives. You will lose money if that happens. (This is true of any trading strategy.)
2. You buy the winning stock at the wrong time or at a poor price, which causes an immediate loss in the position. (This is also true of any trading strategy.)
3. You chose the wrong stock. (Also true of any trading strategy.)

To avoid buying the wrong stock at the wrong time, trading practice is required. After you have made dozens of trades, your trading skills will improve. Never think that you can breeze into the options market without practicing and expect to make money using this strategy or any other.

This may sound harsh, but it's true. I've been to too many option seminars where they charge a hefty fee and convince students that "anyone" can make money trading options after a few days of training. Not true!

Although the Test Trading Strategy works on most days, it still takes practice and skill to choose the right stock and sell for a profit. As the old saying goes, "Practice makes perfect." It also takes patience. It's essential that you wait until you have clearly identified a winner before buying. I understand that it is frustrating to watch a stock price climb higher when you do not yet own a position. However, rushing to buy before the uptrend is established is a mistake.

Not Every Day Is a Winner

It's important to remember that if you are trading options, there will also be boring days. On some days, it's not possible to find a stock that fits your criteria. On other days, no stocks are moving at all and volatility is quite low. When that happens, consider sitting on the sidelines or temporarily changing strategies.

Do not feel compelled to trade every day. There are some days when nothing is working, no winning stocks have emerged, and the market is as dull as dishwater. As Jesse Livermore used to say, "Not even a skunk can make a scent."

End-of-Day Evaluation

By now, you should have a pretty good idea of how the Test Trading Strategy works. You have set up the test trading account in advance, tracked the biggest winners on the days when the market environment was favorable, and perhaps already made some real trades.

After the trading day ends, many traders stop thinking about the market. This is a common mistake. In fact, one of the most important parts of the day is reviewing how the day went. It only takes a few minutes.

This is when you evaluate your profits or losses and take brief notes. Keep a record of what happened during the market day for future reference. You can create an "evaluation form" to make it easier to track the market's performance.

You also want to track how the market reacts on days when the Federal Reserve meets, a holiday, or the day earnings are announced. You can get these answers and more by keeping notes every day. By keeping records, you may be able to notice when the market is acting irrationally.

In addition, although it's a lot more fun to remember only your profitable days, it's best to be brutally honest with yourself, especially if you are losing money. It's better to accept the fact you are financially bleeding early rather than late. You also want to take the time to reflect on any mistakes that were made, and take steps to

avoid repeating them. There is nothing wrong with making mistakes—repeating those mistakes is inexcusable.

> *Note:* If you still have questions about the Test Trading
> Strategy, go to Chapter 9, where I provide additional answers.

. . . .

In the next chapter, I'll introduce a quick and easy way to evaluate
the overall market environment. Of course, you can use technical
indicators to do this, but by using a new method, Stock Market
Behavior Analysis, you have another way of reading the market.
That will give you clues to tell you whether you should enter the
market or if it's too dangerous to participate.

6

Stock Market Behavior Analysis

Many traders and investors never fully understand how the stock market works. To the novice, the stock market appears to be logical, straightforward, and fair. After all, that's what everyone tells you, and what is taught at most financial institutions.

The stock market is a lot more complex than many realize. On some trading days, the market moves in unpredictable and unexpected directions, and on other days it meanders aimlessly. The changes in the price of stocks and indexes are often fueled by computer programs (algorithms, or algos) that trade large stock volume. Other contributors to market volatility are breaking news, or comments and actions by the Federal Reserve (the Fed).

Think of the market as a complicated puzzle that changes every day, similar to trying to solve a Rubik's Cube. To make sense of a nonsensical market, it's essential that you learn to read the overall market environment correctly. If you could accomplish this task, you would have a huge edge over other traders who enter the market without a clue about what is truly happening.

Because so many traders don't know how to read the overall market, they often don't realize when the market is too risky and should be avoided, or when it's a good time to own positions. In this chapter, you will learn how to evaluate the market. It is an essential skill that you need in order to make money in the market.

How to Read and Analyze the Market Environment

As you probably know, there are three primary ways to analyze the stock market. The most well known is *fundamental analysis*, where investors study a company's balance sheet and analyze earnings and other fundamental information to find strong companies with positive growth potential. Long-term buy-and-hold investors primarily use this method.

The second way of analyzing the stock market is *technical analysis*. This is the preferred method of short-term traders, including options traders who study chart patterns and technical indicators and *oscillators* to identify underlying stocks that are moving higher or lower. By using support and resistance, technicians try to identify trends and recognize when a stock is making a top or bottom.

The third method used to analyze the stock market is *sentiment analysis*. This method involves studying investor behavior to identify when the market is overbought or oversold. It's a contrarian method, which means that when investors are extremely bullish, sentiment analysts believe it's time to sell. And if investors are extremely bearish, then it's time to buy.

Each method has advantages and disadvantages. Unfortunately for stock and options traders, technical analysis is not easy to use and understand, and it often gives false signals, costing traders money. Although there are technical analysts who are experts at interpreting indicators and oscillators, many retail traders struggle with using technical analysis to know when to enter or exit option or stock positions.

Stock Market Behavior Analysis

After years of experimenting and testing various strategies and methods, I created a fast and easy way of analyzing the market. It's called Stock Market Behavior Analysis™. If you have never heard of it, it's because this is the first time it's being introduced.

If you are open to new ideas, and are willing to learn something unique, you are in the right place. No matter which method you use to analyze the market, you should find that Stock Market Behavior Analysis will enhance the methods you are already using.

Don't get me wrong: I did not say that Stock Market Behavior Analysis is better than traditional methods such as technical analysis, but it is different. As you learn more about it, you will find it doesn't have to replace the methods you are already using.

In other words, if you use technical analysis to buy and sell options, you should keep doing what works for you. But if you're willing to enhance your trading experience and see the market differently than you did before, you may want to give this new approach a chance.

What It Is and Isn't

Stock Market Behavior Analysis is not technical analysis. It is a simple method of quickly reading the market using chart pattern names that I made up (so it isn't confused with technical analysis).

The purpose of this method is to give you a brief snapshot of the current market. If you have the time, it is recommended that you learn and read about technical analysis, which gives you actionable signals when to buy and sell. Stock Market Behavior Analysis only gives you an overview of the overall market, and no actionable signals.

Note: If you want actionable signals to help you with buy and sell decisions, use traditional technical analysis. If you are not familiar with this method, there are hundreds of books on the subject. I urge you to study more if you are looking for actionable technical signals.

The Importance of the Market Environment

Before you place an options trade, the first action you should take is to evaluate the overall market environment. This is similar to pilots checking weather conditions before taking off in an airplane. This reduces the chance that their passengers will be in danger.

And yet, every single day in the stock market, traders rarely check overall market conditions before buying. They probably didn't check the futures market, and don't have a clue about whether the market is safe or dangerous for their money. Put another way, they are going to fly blind without any idea of the environment they are entering. Believe me, every market day is different.

Therefore, before making a trade and to avoid losing money, it is a good idea to evaluate the current market environment. On some days, you will run into nasty conditions, which means you may want to limit or avoid trading altogether. On other days, the market skies will be blue, and you can make money without too much effort.

Bottom line: Correctly reading the market, especially in the first 15 to 30 minutes of the trading day, is one of the keys to success in trading. Once you correctly identify market conditions, you can create strategies that match what is happening in real life.

Stock Market Behavior Patterns

The stock market exhibits several specific behavior patterns that are repeated every single day. The key is to identify which behavior patterns will help you decide whether to buy, sell, or take the day off.

Once you start to recognize these patterns, it will open up an entirely new way of seeing the market. With practice, it will be easy to identify them each day. Fortunately, most of the behavior patterns are easy to spot.

For each behavior pattern, I created an easily remembered name. The names are easier to memorize and more fun than the technical patterns favored by technicians. Beginner traders should find the names a lot less intimidating but helpful in identifying current market conditions.

Each behavior pattern you will learn can be used with individual stocks or ETFs such as SPY or QQQ. To help you identify the different behavior patterns, I've included a screenshot of each behavior pattern.

The faster you can recognize market behaviors after the market opens, the easier it will be to create a successful trading plan. Some market behaviors are so dangerous that you should not trade at all, similar to flying into a thunderstorm on takeoff. On most days, the market will display multiple behavior patterns, especially right after the market opens.

Note: Each of the patterns will be displayed on a one-minute daily chart, as it gives the best outline of the behavior pattern. You are free to use any time period you wish, but the one-minute daily chart is best for visualizing the behavior pattern. Keep in mind you are not trading using a one-minute chart, but instead you are using it to identify behavior patterns.

Caveat and Clarification

Once again, although the charts will resemble the ones used in technical analysis, they are not the same. If you use technical analysis, the preferred method of most traders, you will put indicators and oscillators on a chart. The charts in this chapter do not include indicators or oscillators.

Stock Market Behavior Analysis is a nontechnical way of looking at the overall market. It gives you a directional road map to help you get an overview of the overall market; it does not give actionable signals. If anything, the patterns confirm what you have already learned in the test trading account. Identifying one of the behavior patterns can help you create a trading plan or script.

> *Note:* In the first 15 minutes, it's usually difficult to identify the correct behavior pattern, so be patient as the bulls and bears fight for control. Your goal is to eventually find which behavior pattern is dominant and then match that with what you learned in the test trading account.

Feel free to track any index or stock using Stock Market Behavior Analysis. I suggest that you start tracking the exchange-traded fund SPY each day.

Finally, you may want to read this chapter slowly (and with frequent breaks) since there is so much new information that will take time to understand and digest.

The Steamroller

And now, let's introduce one of the most powerful behavior patterns on the planet, and my personal favorite: the *Steamroller.*

You will probably enjoy the Steamroller behavior pattern because it can bring the most money with the least amount of effort.

In fact, if all you did was to wait and trade only the Steamroller, you could probably make a good living as a trader. Because the Steamroller is so important, it's essential that you recognize it when one appears.

One unique characteristic of the Steamroller is that it starts slowly and then builds up power and strength during the day, rejecting all attempts to slow or reverse it. The power of the Steamroller is so great that it is nearly unstoppable.

There are two types of Steamrollers: the *Bullish Steamroller* and *Bearish Steamroller*.

The Bullish Steamroller

As the name suggests, when you look at the Bullish Steamroller on a one-minute chart (a one-minute chart is my preference because it's easy to see the behavior pattern), you will see a strong uptrend that begins slowly in the morning and then builds strength as the day progresses. By noon ET, it is overpowering (with only occasional minor pullbacks).

On some days, you can identify a Bullish Steamroller in the first hour (but not always). Often, a Bullish Steamroller can be recognized when the market is very strong right from the opening (over 1 percent on the Dow or S&P 500, i.e., SPX), and gains power as the day progresses. Once it gets going, the Bullish Steamroller is relentless right until the close.

Typically, a Bullish Steamroller develops in the futures market, pointing to a strong bullish opening. Nevertheless, not all strong openings turn into a Bullish Steamroller, but many do. If you can identify a Bullish Steamroller before the market opens, and if you jump on the trend early enough, you can make some serious money by trading this behavior pattern.

There are also days when the Bullish Steamroller develops later in the day. For example, the market might meander for the first hour, and in midmorning turn into a strong Bullish Steamroller, and then "steamroll" everyone in its path.

Figure 6.1 shows a one-minute chart of a Bullish Steamroller behavior pattern.

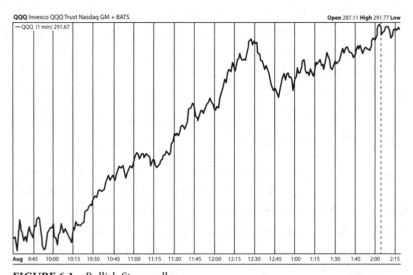

FIGURE 6.1   Bullish Steamroller
Source: Chart courtesy of StockCharts.com

Here are several Bullish Steamroller observations:

1. Technicians might identify the Bullish Steamroller as an uptrend, but it's not just any uptrend. It is one of the most powerful uptrends in the market. It may begin slowly and then build up strength all day and into the afternoon. It will mow down any attempt by short sellers to stall or reverse its direction. Although there may be turbulence along the way, the Bullish Steamroller gets slowly stronger as the day progresses. That's how you know it's a true Steamroller.

2. The Bullish Steamroller can be a huge moneymaker if it is identified early. It tends to lift all the leading stocks higher.

The chances of a reversal are slim when it is a true Bullish Steamroller.

3. Don't make the common mistake of proclaiming a Bullish Steamroller too early, because many times the market starts off strongly but then loses steam within the first hour. To be a true Bullish Steamroller, the indexes (or individual stocks) must continue to move higher with only temporary pullbacks.

4. *Warning*: The biggest risk when you are trading the Bullish Steamroller occurs when there is a sudden Intraday Reversal. A Bullish Steamroller rarely reverses, but if it happens, it's usually due to negative breaking news. The odds of a reversal are slim because nearly everyone, including institutions, day traders, investors, hedge funds, and algos, has been buying into the strong uptrend.

If you correctly identify a Bullish Steamroller, buying calls on individual stocks or ETFs will be a profitable venture. I suspect you could do well by trading calls on the days when a Bullish Steamroller develops.

The Bearish Steamroller

The Bearish Steamroller is an extremely strong and powerful behavior pattern that ultimately forms an unstoppable downtrend that usually continues all day. With a Bearish Steamroller, you should be patient and more cautious than when trading a Bullish Steamroller.

The reason for caution is simple: Nearly everyone connected to the financial markets wants the market to move higher. So when the market is moving lower and a Bearish Steamroller develops, the whole financial establishment is rooting for a reversal. Unlike the Bullish Steamroller, when it's relatively easy to make money, you have to work hard to make money with the Bearish Steamroller.

For example, although the Bearish Steamroller may be in a strong downtrend, at different times during the day, especially when it is first developing, buy-on-the-dip entities, with help from financial institutions, may try to reverse the downtrend and push the market higher.

If it's a true Bearish Steamroller, however, the attempts will fail. Nevertheless, it's not always easy to hold onto winning put positions while getting temporarily head-faked with rallies.

Figure 6.2 shows a one-minute chart of a Bearish Steamroller behavior pattern.

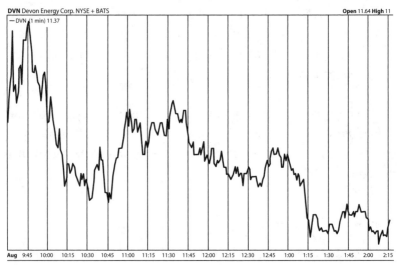

FIGURE 6.2   Bearish Steamroller
Source: Chart courtesy of StockCharts.com

Here are some Bearish Steamroller observations:

1. A Bearish Steamroller can be a tricky animal because it exhibits a lot of unpredictable behavior as the market moves lower. If you can identify a Bearish Steamroller early and calmly hold your position while the market (or stock) twists

and turns, you can do well. The odds are good the market will move lower all day, and even lower into the close. It is not certain this will happen, but if it's a true Bearish Steamroller, it will.

2. If the indexes are down by more than .75 percent in the futures market, there's a good likelihood the market will open lower (but there are no guarantees until the opening bell).

3. The next clue that a Bearish Steamroller might be the real deal is if the market is still weak after it opens, perhaps lower by .75 percent to 1 percent. After an initial period of confusion and turbulence, the Bearish Steamroller typically results in lower prices as it enters into a slow but powerful downtrend. It will repel all attempts to rally and often plunges right into the last hour of the day.

4. The Bearish Steamroller, if identified correctly, can be very profitable for bearish traders who own puts. The first big test for the Bearish Steamroller is when midday arrives. Because volatility is usually lower in the middle of the trading day, it's easier for financial institutions and bullish traders to push the market higher. Watch closely how the indexes react during this time period. If the rallies fail, that is a strong clue that a true Bearish Steamroller is occurring.

5. *Warning*: Be careful not to make this common mistake: Many bearish traders will proclaim a Bearish Steamroller too soon, perhaps within the first half hour, and then buy puts. Too often, they are shocked when the downtrend reverses direction. It's important to be patient and to wait for confirmation before buying puts. You do not want to buy too early and get trapped in a losing position.

6. *Warning*: On occasion, there may be positive breaking news, which can cause the indexes to suddenly reverse direction. There is no way to predict when breaking news

will occur, so be sure that you have a plan to handle a potential Intraday Reversal.

If you can identify a Bearish Steamroller, buying SPY and QQQ puts can be very profitable. Experienced traders can buy puts on individual stocks, but for beginners, it's recommended that you start with buying puts on ETFs.

And now, let's take a look at other behavior patterns.

Rocky Road

One of the most common, and risky, market behavior patterns is the Rocky Road. This chaotic pattern is fraught with risk, and it shows up often on a chart. Rocky Road occurs when the bulls and bears are having a tug-of-war with no clear winner.

Here is a one-minute chart of a Rocky Road behavior pattern:

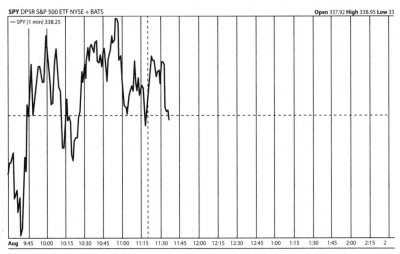

FIGURE 6.3   Rocky Road
Source: Chart courtesy of StockCharts.com

Here are several observations about Rocky Road:

1. The Rocky Road pattern makes multiple reversals, moving from a high to a low to a high (shown in Figure 6.3). Beginners who are not aware of the Rocky Road pattern will probably enter at the wrong time and get chopped up.

2. Rocky Road can occur at any time during the day, but it often appears early, within the first half hour after the market opens, and lasts until the index or stock moves decisively higher or lower. One characteristic of a Rocky Road is that it usually doesn't remain in that pattern all day.

3. When the Rocky Road behavior pattern appears, it is a clue that the market is confused and indecisive. Unless you're an excellent market timer, or a *scalper*, many traders will lose money trading this chaotic pattern.

4. If the unpredictable Rocky Road pattern appears on a chart, it's wise to avoid trading. You must know when to hold, fold, or walk away from the computer. Basically, the pattern says that the bulls and bears are fighting for control. Because no trend has been established, the market moves higher and lower like a roller coaster. This is a difficult trading environment.

5. Although a Rocky Road pattern doesn't usually last all day, it sometimes lasts longer than expected, and on those days, you do not have to trade. Most of the time, however, a Rocky Road resolves itself by the afternoon and breaks out in one direction or the other. You should observe, but not trade, a Rocky Road pattern until it makes up its mind where it wants to go.

Extreme Openings: Spike Up and Spike Down

Spike Up

A Spike Up means that an index or stock moves up so high and fast at the open that it displays a vertical line on a one-minute chart. Many inexperienced traders try to make money by chasing after an index or stock that spikes up, hoping to jump on its coattails and ride it higher. Big mistake.

While inexperienced traders may get trapped in their long positions, experienced traders may bet against the spike. *Advice:* Don't get trapped in a spike! In fact, don't get involved at all until you gain more experience.

Figure 6.4 shows a one-minute chart of the Spike Up behavior pattern.

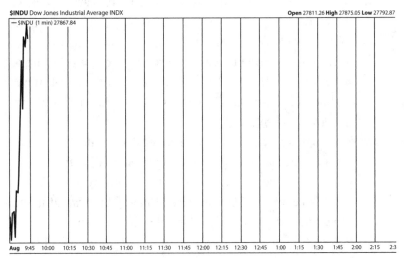

FIGURE 6.4   Spike Up
Source: Chart courtesy of StockCharts.com

Here are some observations about the Spike Up:

1. A Spike Up is a warning sign that signals a reversal is likely. Often, after spiking higher at the open, the stock or index may move sideways, and often it reverses direction.
2. If an individual stock rises by a huge percentage (i.e., 8 or 9 percent) right after the market opens, that is a Spike Up. Although the extreme rally may continue longer, the odds of a reversal are likely. *Advice:* Do not chase a stock or index that has spiked up by a large amount. If you buy calls after the stock makes such an extreme move, you are probably buying at an unreasonably high price, and at the wrong time.
3. If you are fortunate enough to own calls during a Spike Up, you may consider selling those calls, either in halves or all, into the euphoria. It's possible the rally will continue, however, so it's a choice only you can make.
4. A Spike Up may occur at any time during the trading day, although soon after the open is when a reversal is most likely.

Spike Up versus *Bullish Steamroller*: It's essential that you recognize the difference between a stock or index that spikes up at the open and a stock or index that is moving slowly higher, and perhaps turns into a Bullish Steamroller later in the day.

On a chart, both vertical lines may look similar. However, here is the difference: A stock or index that has spiked higher moves incredibly fast. A Bullish Steamroller, however, develops slowly at first and builds up strength as the day progresses.

Now let's take a look at the opposite behavior.

Spike Down

While stocks and indexes that spike up are cheered by most traders and investors, a Spike Down causes anxiety. Often, before the
market opens, the S&P 500 (SPX) futures are trading lower, and the
indexes may spike down right after the market opens.

When the indexes drop fast and hard at open, it creates a vertical downtrend on a chart. It's possible, but not guaranteed, that a
stock or index will stall and reverse within minutes. After the open,
if there is a spike down, be on the lookout for a sudden reversal.

Figure 6.5 shows a one-minute chart of a Spike Down behavior
pattern.

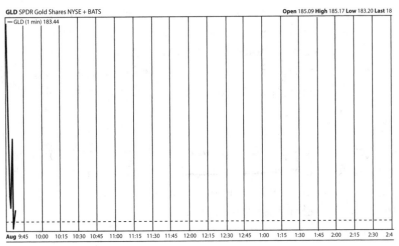

FIGURE 6.5   Spike Down
Source: Chart courtesy of StockCharts.com

Here are observations about the Spike Down:

1.   If you own puts during a Spike Down, it's often a wise decision to sell those puts, all or in halves, into the panic and
fear. Typically, the fear and panic don't last long, so it's wise

to take the put profits early. A Spike Down causes implied volatility on puts to skyrocket.

2. If a stock plunges by a large amount (i.e., 8 or 9 percent) right as the market opens, although the sell-off may continue longer, the odds of a reversal are likely. *Advice:* Do not chase a stock or index that has spiked down. If you buy puts on the way down, you are probably buying at a high price, and at the wrong time. That is a money-losing proposition.

3. Be sure that you recognize the difference between a stock or index that has spiked down and a Bearish Steamroller. A stock that has spiked lower moves quickly, while a Bearish Steamroller continues to slowly decline throughout the day.

4. A Spike Down may occur at any time during the trading day, although soon after the open is when a reversal is most likely.

Sideways Sucker

One of the most commonly observed behavior patterns is the Sideways Sucker, also known as *consolidation* to technical analysts. Unlike the Rocky Road, which makes large, more extreme moves, a Sideways Sucker makes smaller zigzagging moves but in a tight, controlled environment. That makes it nearly impossible to trade (unless you like to lose money).

Figure 6.6 shows a one-minute chart of the Sideways Sucker behavior pattern.

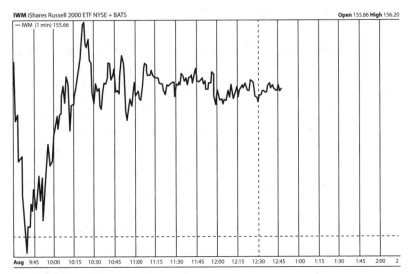

IWM iShares Russell 2000 ETF NYSE + BATS   Open 155.86 High 156.20
— IWM (1 min) 155.66

FIGURE 6.6 Sideways Sucker
Source: Chart courtesy of StockCharts.com

Here are several observations about the Sideways Sucker behavior pattern:

1. It's called a Sideways Sucker pattern because if you trade during this pattern, the odds are good you are making a sucker play. Why? Because the moves are so small, it's difficult to come out ahead. Eventually, the stock or index will break out of the sideways pattern, but it's impossible to predict when or in what direction. It's best to wait patiently on the sidelines and not trade until the market (or stock) gives a clear signal.

2. It's very common for the market to move into a sleepy Sideways Sucker pattern during midday. Volume and volatility often decrease during this time, so patience is required. At the same time, be on guard because the market can abruptly move out of the sideways pattern without warning.

3. A Sideways Sucker pattern is so unpredictable, it's usually best to not trade it at all when one appears on the chart. Find something else to buy, or take a break.

Strong Rally

A Strong Rally is a common behavior pattern that appears as an uptrend. The interesting part about a Strong Rally is that it has the potential to turn into a Bullish Steamroller. The stronger the market moves higher, the more likely it will continue in the same direction.

Watch how it reacts to pullbacks. If it briefly reverses direction but keeps moving consistently higher, that is a clue that the rally will continue, perhaps even gaining strength.

Figure 6.7 shows a one-minute chart of a Strong Rally behavior pattern.

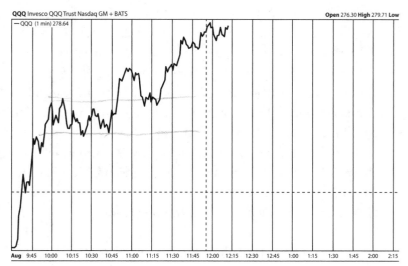

FIGURE 6.7 Strong Rally
Source: Chart courtesy of StockCharts.com

Here are a couple of observations about the Strong Rally:

1. A Strong Rally is a big moneymaker when you own calls and entered early. Because of the risk of an Intraday Reversal, closely watch your call positions throughout the day.
2. Do not fight a strong uptrend by buying puts, especially in a bull market. It's common for bearish traders to lose huge sums of money betting against strong rallies, ignoring the stock market behavior patterns. There are times when you can trade against the trend, but not when there is a Strong Rally that develops out of the starting gate.

Strong Sell-off

A Strong Sell-off is a common behavior pattern that appears as a downtrend. An interesting observation about a Strong Sell-off is that bullish institutions and other financial entities may try to reverse the negative trajectory with a "bull raid." That often results in mild turbulence after the open. If the bull raids are unsuccessful, however, the indexes and stocks will continue falling.

On some days, a Strong Sell-off turns into a Bearish Steamroller. If you are long with calls, you must exercise sound risk management skills to limit losses. Otherwise, look out below! (Obviously, it's a lot more profitable if you own puts when there is a Strong Sell-off.)

Figure 6.8 shows a one-minute chart of a Strong Sell-off behavior pattern.

Here is an observation about the Strong Sell-off:

1. A Strong Sell-off can be difficult to manage because of the multiple head-fake reversals. As the market declines, nervous put owners are often tempted to abandon their prof-

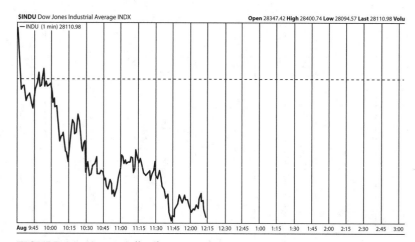

$INDU Dow Jones Industrial Average INDX   **Open** 28347.42 **High** 28400.74 **Low** 28094.57 **Last** 28110.98 **Volu**

FIGURE 6.8 Strong Sell-off
Source: Chart courtesy of StockCharts.com

itable positions. Put owners who are not easily frightened into abandoning their positions can do well if they hold as the sell-off continues.

Slow Rally

A Slow Rally begins its upside move so quietly that it is often ignored, or not even noticed. The slow and lumbering rally is not a sign of weakness. In fact, it could be a sign of strength as an ever-increasing number of financial institutions and investors buy into the rally.

At times, a Slow Rally develops into a very powerful uptrend, and may even turn into a Bullish Steamroller later in the day. This unassuming behavior pattern provides many profitable opportunities, and it should not be ignored.

Figure 6.9 shows a one-minute chart of a Slow Rally behavior pattern.

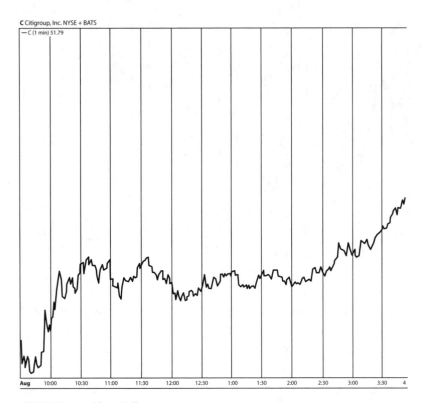

FIGURE 6.9   Slow Rally
Source: Chart courtesy of StockCharts.com

Here is an observation about the Slow Rally:

1. There is always the possibility that a Slow Rally will falter as the day progresses. That is one reason why it is important to watch this pattern closely and give it enough time to develop. The good news is that there are probably many individual stocks that are moving higher with the slow rally. That means there are a lot of opportunities to make money buying calls.

Slow Sell-off

A Slow Sell-off also begins quietly without attracting too much attention. Because the sell-off is so unassuming, the market really could go in either direction. Neither the Slow Rally nor the Slow Sell-off is strong enough to attract the attention of most traders, at least at first. Even if the market is not cooperative, look at individual stocks for potential trading opportunities.

Sometimes a Slow Sell-off turns into a powerful downtrend and evolves into a Bearish Steamroller later in the day. It's smart to watch and wait before committing to either side. A Slow Sell-off can undergo unpredictable moves as Mr. Market tries to find its way.

Figure 6.10 shows a one-minute chart of a Slow Sell-off behavior pattern.

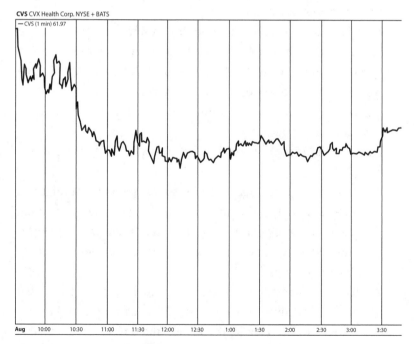

FIGURE 6.10   Slow Sell-off
Source: Chart courtesy of StockCharts.com

Here is an observation about the Slow Sell-off:

1. Slow Sell-offs are susceptible to reversals, especially on low volume. Buy-on-the-dippers often initiate positions during the sell-off, hoping the lower price trend ends. Patience is the key to trading this behavior pattern.

Flat, Weak, or Indecisive Pattern

This behavior pattern can put you to sleep. It's a trendless behavior pattern that appears to be going nowhere. When this boring pattern appears after the open, it is a clue the market is indecisive. Don't let down your guard, because a flat market eventually breaks out of its funk and chooses a direction.

If it's a flat and weak market opening, you may want to look for individual stocks to trade. It also might be a good day to shut down the computer and find something else to do. There is no rule that says you must trade every day, and in fact, you shouldn't.

Figure 6.11 shows a one-minute chart of a Flat, Weak, or Indecisive behavior pattern.

Here are observations about the Flat, Weak, or Indecisive pattern:

1. Although a Flat, Weak, or Indecisive opening is similar to a Sideways Sucker, the difference is that an indecisive or flat market or stock can last all day, while a Sideways Sucker is temporary. With either behavior pattern, you get many false starts and stops.
2. It's usually best to avoid trading a stock or index that is flat or weak or gives conflicting signals. Search for other individual stocks to trade, if you can find any, or don't trade at all that day.

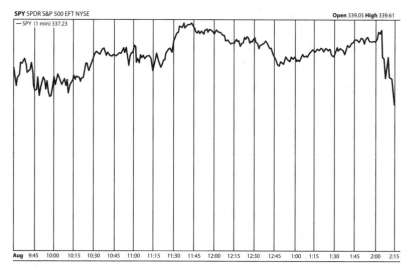

FIGURE 6.11 Flat, Weak, or Indecisive
Source: Chart courtesy of StockCharts.com

Intraday Reversals

Now that you've been introduced to the most common behavior patterns, it's time to learn how to spot major Intraday Reversals. Although temporary reversals are common, a major Intraday Reversal occurs less often.

When a reversal does occur, it signals that the current trend has changed, at least for that day. Often, the new trend that appears will carry over into the next day, but not always. Still, whenever an Intraday Reversal is detected, pay attention.

The two main Intraday Reversals are what I call a Failed Sell-off and a Failed Rally.

Failed Sell-off (Bullish)

A Failed Sell-off can be fun and profitable to trade if timed correctly (which takes a lot of practice to do successfully). This pattern is exciting for bullish traders who like to buy on dips. Just when the bears think they are victorious, there is a rush of buying that stops the sell-off in its track, and the indexes (or stocks) begin to rally. The Failed Sell-off, if it continues, is extremely bullish.

Figure 6.12 shows a one-minute chart of a Failed Sell-off behavior pattern.

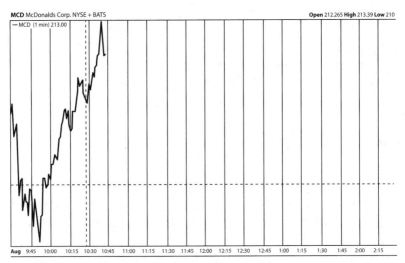

FIGURE 6.12   Failed Sell-off
Source: Chart courtesy of StockCharts.com

Here are several observations about the Failed Sell-off:

1. The Failed Sell-off is a bullish signal, and the odds are good the uptrend will continue (but there are no guarantees).
2. Failed Sell-offs are notable because as the indexes fall after the market opens, bearish traders, who bet the market will keep falling, are lured into taking bearish positions (they get

caught in the so-called *bear trap*). Then they are shocked when the market suddenly reverses direction.

3. Anytime there is a sell-off, be prepared for a reversal. A Failed Sell-off can bring excellent profits on the long side, but wait until after the reversal has been completed (the market stalls, reverses, and breaks out) before going long. Patience and good timing skills are the keys to making money with a Failed Sell-off.

Failed Rally (Bearish)

You always learn more from rallies than from sell-offs. Therefore, if a rally starts off strong but then fails and reverses direction, that is a bearish signal that needs to be watched closely. It may signal a significant trend change.

Figure 6.13 shows a one-minute chart of a Failed Rally behavior pattern.

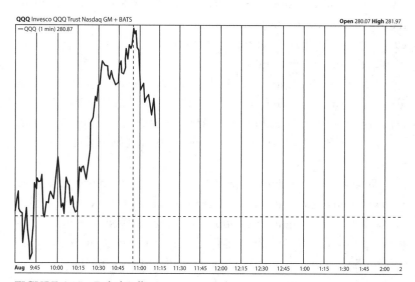

FIGURE 6.13   Failed Rally
Source: Chart courtesy of StockCharts.com

Here is an observation about the Failed Rally:

1. The initial rally will attract bullish investors who bought at or near the top (the so-called *bull trap*), and who continue to buy right until the rally stalls and signals a reversal. If the reversal holds, it's likely the bears will take over, at least temporarily.

Questions and Answers: Stock Market Behavior Analysis

Now that you have finished learning about Stock Market Behavior Analysis, let's answer a few questions.

QUESTION: *Why is it so important to study the overall market?* Evaluating the market environment is important to your success as a trader. If you waltz into the stock or options market without evaluating market conditions, you are already at a disadvantage. It's not easy to be a successful options trader, so it's essential that you try to gain every possible advantage.

When you think about it, the behavior patterns you just learned about are simply another way of identifying and evaluating the current trend, something that legendary trader Jesse Livermore was famous for. (Go to Chapter 12 to read about Livermore's trading tactics.)

This is what Livermore wrote: "I think it was a long step forward in my trading education when I realized at last that when old Mr. Partridge kept on telling the other customers, 'Well, you know this is a bull market!' he really meant to tell them that the big money was not in individual fluctuations but in the main movements—that is, not in reading the tape but in sizing up the entire market and its trend."

In reality, it was old Mr. Partridge who correctly identified the market trend, and recommended not trading against it. Livermore realized that if he could correctly identify the overall market environment and be on the same side as the trend, his chances of success would increase.

For the rest of his life, Livermore was a "trend trader," but unfortunately, just identifying and following a trend is not enough to ensure success. This is a lesson that traders learn every time the trend suddenly reverses without warning, leaving them with an unwanted position.

QUESTION: *Can you predict when there will be an Intraday Reversal?*
It is nearly impossible to predict an Intraday Reversal, especially when it is the result of news. However, there are technical analysts who use oscillators or indicators to predict which stocks might reverse. Technical indicators are the tool of choice to recognize potential reversals.

One of the problems with technical analysis is that it produces many false signals. Nevertheless, indicators and oscillators work often enough to make them useful to those who know how to use them properly.

Many traders try to time the market by betting on when a top or bottom is reached. That skill is extremely hard to get right. One reason for learning trend strategies in this book is that following a trend is easier than trying to predict Intraday Reversals.

QUESTION: *Is Stock Market Behavior Analysis another version of technical analysis?*
No! I thought this was made clear, but if it wasn't, I'd like to emphasize again: Stock Market Behavior Analysis is a simple method I created that analyzes stock market behavior using a one-minute chart. It is not technical analysis. The only similarity is that both use charting software.

Stock Market Behavior Analysis is used only to get a quick visual overview of the market to help create a trade plan for the day and to help identify high-risk market conditions.

This method also helps traders evaluate whether to buy a stock or ETF and also helps identify trends. Based on what the chart is saying, you may get clues about what to do next. This method is easier to use than technical analysis, and it is designed to evaluate stock and market behavior, and not to give actionable signals. It is also useful for traders who don't have time to learn technical analysis.

· · · · · · · ·

Congratulations for spending the time to learn a new way of analyzing the market. Not many traders are willing to try something new, so I give you credit for doing so. I hope you found it valuable.

In Part Three, you will learn about other trading strategies, including how to trade two of the most popular ETFs: SPY and QQQ, as well as learning about other strategies that involve increased risk. If you're looking for something a little different, then Part Three should meet your needs.

PART THREE

OTHER TRADING STRATEGIES

Now that you have learned about the Test Trading Strategy, in Part Three we'll discuss more traditional options strategies, including trading SPY and QQQ. In addition, you will be introduced to "off-the-wall" option strategies that may involve more risk, such as countertrend strategies and long shots. Finally, questions about options strategies and trading tactics will be answered.

Anyone looking for sophisticated ways to increase profits by trading options should find a number of ideas in this part.

7

Trade SPY and QQQ

In this chapter, you will learn strategies for buying ETF calls and puts with a focus on SPY and QQQ. As always, if you are on the right side of the trend, you can make good money. But if you are on the wrong side, you can incur serious losses.

As you know, the strategy of most traders is to predict the direction of SPY and QQQ (or hundreds of other ETFs), by buying options that fit their viewpoint. Many err by holding the calls and puts all the way until expiration.

As you may recall, I never recommend holding calls or puts until they expire. In addition, although predicting the future direction of ETFs is a popular strategy, it's difficult to win, even when you are helped with technical indicators and oscillators.

Nevertheless, it is possible to make money trading ETFs such as SPY and QQQ, and in this chapter, we will explore some of the ways to do so.

Which Is Better to Trade: Stocks or ETFs?

Many traders want to know whether they should trade individual stocks or ETFs. The answer is that it's a personal preference. The best advice is to start by learning how to make money buying calls on individual stocks, and after that, learn to trade ETFs. Later you can practice buying SPY or QQQ puts, which can be very profitable during downtrends or bear markets.

> *Note:* Although SPY and QQQ are mentioned repeatedly in this book, there are several other ETFs you could follow and trade. Examples include the Russell 2000 (IWM) and the Dow Jones Industrial Average Index (DIA), to name a couple.

SPY and QQQ are ideal trading vehicles for calls and puts because these two ETFs are liquid, not leveraged, and are actively traded, and their options have a tight bid-ask spread. If you are new to trading ETFs, start by trading options on SPY and QQQ. You can always look at other ETFs when you gain more experience.

Unfortunately, many ETFs are unsuitable for trading options because the market for these securities is so thin. With many ETFs, it's difficult for option buyers to get a fair deal. In particular, stay away from leveraged (2x, 3x ETFs) or illiquid ETFs such as the ones that buy volatility or have low trading volume. They are easy to buy, but difficult to exit.

Buying SPY and QQQ Calls Using the Test Trading Strategy

You have already learned how to use the Test Trading Strategy to buy individual stocks. In this chapter, you will learn how to set up to trade SPY and QQQ. The advantage of using the test trading account for ETFs is that the setup is quick and easy. It usually takes less than a minute to buy ETFs in the test trading account.

If you liked the Test Trading Strategy for individual stocks, you should like using it with ETFs. Again, it's a personal choice whether you want to use it or not. If interested, keep reading!

> *Note:* If your brokerage firm doesn't have a simulated trading platform, you can still use the following strategies by adding and monitoring SPY and QQQ on your Watch List and purchasing calls or puts when you have identified the trend. In addition, use technical analysis to determine when to enter or exit.

Now we're going to make a paper money purchase of five SPY and QQQ calls after the market opens. (We must wait until after the market opens at 9:30 a.m. ET to trade options, even in the test trading account.)

1. Make a Paper Money Purchase of Five SPY Calls

Right after the market opens, place a market order to buy five SPY at-the-money calls in the test trading account. Use a one-to-two-month expiration date. The order should be filled immediately since it's a market order.

> *Example:* Let's say that on April 7, SPY is trading at $280.34 per share in the premarket. After the market opens, in the test trading account, place a market order to buy five SPY calls at a strike price of $280 (at the money).

Select a one-to-two-month expiration date (in this example, select May 15 or June 18, which is one to two months away). The April expiration date is too early for our purposes since it is less than one month.

Note: Once again, the criteria used for test trades are different from those used when making real trades. For example, you rarely enter a market order when making a real trade. You almost always use a limit order.

2. Make a Paper Money Purchase of Five QQQ Calls

You will now make a similar test trade for QQQ. It's April 7, and QQQ is trading at $201.89 per share. Buy five QQQ calls at a strike price of 202 (at the money) with a minimum one-month expiration date.

Buying Calls in the Real Brokerage Account

Now that you have set up your test trading account to include SPY and QQQ calls as well as shares of stock, you may consider buying calls in the real brokerage account. Keep reading for some clues on when to buy.

Prepare to Buy SPY and QQQ Calls

Although your first choice for making money is to buy calls on individual stocks that are trending higher, there are times when buying SPY or QQQ is a better choice. Keep in mind that buying indexes is not always an easy path to profits.

Because you have identified the winning direction of SPY or QQQ, it is time to make a real trade. If right, the option returns can be very profitable. If wrong, losses can add up quickly, especially if you hold too long. When trading ETFs such as SPY or QQQ, it's essential that you cut your losses quickly when wrong.

If you can afford to buy five or more calls of SPY or QQQ, you can make excellent profits when you correctly call the direction of the overall market. If you don't have enough money, buy fewer options. If you are a beginner, start by buying one call contract.

You can learn a lot by watching SPY and QQQ in the test trading account to see how strong the paper money profits are.

Buy One SPY Call in the Real Brokerage Account

Using a combination of technical analysis, which gives actionable signals, and what you've learned from studying your trades in the test trading account, you may consider buying SPY or QQQ with real money.

Before buying, be sure that you identified the correct behavior pattern (such as the Bullish Steamroller or Strong Rally—see Chapter 6).

If everything looks good based on your analysis, you can go ahead and purchase a SPY or QQQ call position. The number of contracts to buy is up to you, but it should be fewer than five—at least for now. How many calls to buy should also be based on how strong the market appears, and more importantly, on how much cash you are comfortable investing.

If you confirmed the overall market is moving higher, and your analysis confirms there is a strong uptrend, read the hints in the following section, and then buy one call in the real trading account.

A Series of Observations About Buying SPY or QQQ Calls

This is not always an easy trade to make, so read the following hints before risking real money.

Trading Hint #1

If you are right, and the proof is in the profits, you should see gains within a few minutes. Regardless of whether you see that profit, create a time stop and a stop loss, and obey them. If your position is losing money, resist any temptation to add to a losing position, because that is not the path to earning money.

Trading Hint #2

Although you never add to a loser, you can sometimes add to a winning position, especially if you have confirmed it is in a strong uptrend. If you do add, do it only once, and it should be done early, that is, before the ETF breaks out and moves dramatically higher. Admittedly, it is not easy to know when to add to a winner, so if you are not sure, just stick with your original position.

Trading Hint #3

A big mistake that many options traders make is they add to a winning position too late. Adding to winners is a viable plan as long as you add early. But if you keep adding to a winning position too late (after the market has spiked higher), you are chasing, not following.

At some point, the sooner the better, you must stop adding to the winning position and simply watch the profits increase. At that point, you should be thinking of selling or reducing the position, not adding to it.

Trading Hint #4

If the trend remains bullish and profits are increasing, then you obviously are on the right side of the trend. If there isn't a major reversal as the day progresses, the probabilities are favorable that your position will remain profitable most of the day.

Keep in mind that once institutions sniff out a strong uptrend, they will want to pile on and buy. That also happens with retail traders. The only losers will be short sellers, who may be forced to cover their losing short positions. That will fuel the rally even higher.

Trading Hint #5

Because there is always the chance the market could reverse at any time, perhaps due to bad news or bad luck, you must watch your ETF positions closely. This is not the time to go to lunch or do errands. Watch that position until it is sold, as anything can happen at any time during the day.

If you have analyzed the one-minute chart and behavior patterns correctly, it's possible your gains will increase so much you might say to yourself, "I can't believe how much money I made." If that thought crosses your mind, that's a signal to sell at least half of your position. Don't let greed take over your trading. Take the profits when you can, not when you are forced to.

Trading Hint #6

If for some reason you entered at the wrong time and are losing money, do not hesitate to sell the position. Be sure to exit by the end of the day at the latest. Don't forget: Only losers hold losers.

Trading Hint #7

You can hold calls overnight, especially during a bull market, but it's always wise to take option profits sooner rather than later. Options are a wasting asset and lose value as time passes.

Trading Hint #8

Deciding how long to hold a winning ETF option position depends on market conditions and the strength of the rally and whether it's a bull or bear market. In a bull market, you can hold calls longer. If a bear market rally, you should hold calls for a shorter time period.

Trading Hint #9

When you have huge gains, even if a one-day gain, consider selling something. As I like to say, sell it before you lose it. Too many options traders hold winning positions, get greedy, and lose all their profits. The speculative options strategies you learned in this book (buying calls and puts) were not designed to be held until the expiration date, and usually not longer than a week.

Obviously, many options traders disagree, but based on my research and experiments, you will find that option profits often disappear well before the expiration date is reached. When trading options, always be on the side of caution and take profits early. If you like to buy and hold, then invest in stocks. But when trading options, the sooner you take your profits, the better.

Losing potential gains shouldn't bother you because it's money that you never had in the first place. Remember what Sam thought: He was angry about losing money on a trade that he missed. It's a common feeling that should be dismissed.

On the other hand, there's nothing more infuriating than losing money you had made because you failed to take profits when you had the chance. Selling too early will not damage your portfolio. Selling too late will.

If you miss out on bigger gains the next day (or even later on the same day) because you took profits, so be it. There is never an easy answer to the dual dilemma of either selling too soon or selling too late. That is why selling half your position is often a reasonable compromise.

Trading Hint #10

SPY and QQQ are going to be expensive at times because of implied volatility. That is usually not a big concern if you plan to exit the position before the trading day ends.

> *Suggestion:* The more you practice trading with SPY and QQQ, the more knowledge you will gain on what represents a "fair" price for the options. If option premiums were always $4 to $5 for a one-month option, and suddenly options cost $6 or $7, you would know that implied volatility was high. You can make the trade, knowing you are paying more than usual, or not make the trade at all.

Trading Hint #11

If you look at the Dow Jones Industrial Average, it may be trading 1 percent higher, while SPY calls in the test trading account are losing money and in the red. That could be a warning sign that the Dow is not as strong as it appears. It's best when the Dow and SPY calls (or SPX) are aligned.

When you see a divergence between indexes and the stocks in the test trading account, it's possible that a reversal might be on the way. It's not definite there will be a reversal, but it's worth watching.

> *Bottom line:* Be on alert if you see divergences between indexes and stocks.

· · · · · · · ·

I hope these hints help you make buying and selling decisions. It's easy to buy calls on ETFs, but it's not always easy to make money on them. Everything should line up correctly before you actually press the Enter key and make the trade. It doesn't hurt to keep practicing before making a real trade, especially when trading ETFs.

And now, for the first time, let's discuss buying ETF puts. For those with a bearish view of the market, you should find the next section helpful.

Buying SPY and QQQ Puts

I know that some of you have waited a long time for a discussion on buying puts. Thanks for staying around. Buying puts is not for amateurs, and it can take more skills, and patience, to make money on the short side.

The good news is that with proper training and experience, you can make money buying puts, but you have to be more alert, and be willing to cut your losses quickly when things don't go your way.

While excessive bullishness and euphoria can last for weeks, months, or even years, when the market falls, panic and fear don't last very long. Even in the middle of a dreaded bear market, there are numerous one-day rallies that can destroy put buyers.

On the bright side, markets can tumble a lot faster than they rise, providing extra gains for put buyers who get the timing right. There is an added bonus when implied volatility explodes. This nearly never happens with calls. It's amazing how much money you can make when you own puts before the market undergoes a correction or crash.

As always, the key to making money when buying puts is to trade smaller size. Although you can make an occasional long shot trade (deep out-of-the-money put), don't get in the habit of buying cheap puts with little chance of success. No matter how overbought the market might seem, it can get more overbought. That is why you should never short or buy puts if there is a strong uptrend.

Observations About Buying SPY and QQQ Puts

If you want to make money buying SPY and QQQ puts, it's usually wise to wait for a strong downtrend. It takes patience because many financial institutions and investors buy on the dip to make a profit, which may end the downtrend before it picks up steam.

One clue to market behavior is how the market opens. If the major indexes such as the Dow start off lower by more than 1 percent to 1.5 percent, the odds are good that the market will continue falling through the day (with no guarantees because reversals happen often).

Nevertheless, there are many times when a falling market turns into a dreaded plunge, and that is when SPY and QQQ puts can bring big returns. As always, this position must be watched closely, and the profits taken quickly. Be sure to set a time stop, stop loss, or profit target.

Trading Hint #1

Although it's very tempting to buy puts when the market opens lower, that is often a mistake. More than likely, after an initial sell-off, buy-on-the-dip institutions and traders will enter the market with buy orders that can run the indexes higher, at least temporarily.

Trading Hint #2

I've mentioned this before, but it's worth repeating. No matter how bearish you are about the market or a stock, do not plan to hold puts for long. With stocks, you have the luxury of time to allow the position to work. With options, you don't have that luxury.

So sell losers as soon as you decide that your rationale for buying is no longer valid. Thus, if the market is hesitating or the underlying stock or index is underperforming, there is no reason to hold the put position.

It doesn't matter what you "think." The proof is in the profits. If you are losing money when holding puts, you are on the wrong side. It's better to get out with small losses while you still have the chance.

Trading Hint #3

Once again, if you are experiencing a big payoff from owning puts, consider selling at least half the position as soon as the profits reach your target price. If the payout is beyond your wildest dreams, you are probably holding the position too long. Consider selling all those high-priced options. You can always open a newer and smaller position using a different strike price.

Although the returns can be phenomenal on rare occasions, there is always the risk of a bull raid, when the bulls enter the market with firepower and reverse the downtrend. Many unsuspecting bears have been caught on the wrong side of a *bear trap.*

Trading Hint #4

Although it can make sense to follow momentum stocks higher, you should not buy puts on a plunging stock in an attempt to follow momentum to the downside. While stocks can decline even further, the options are probably very costly (high implied volatility). Therefore, it's probably too late to buy puts at this time. Never chase falling stocks.

Buying Puts on Individual Stocks

I know that some of you are anxious to learn how to buy puts on individual stocks. Thanks for your patience. I waited until now to discuss puts on stocks because it's a challenging strategy. The reason is simple: It takes superb timing skills to making money buying puts on stocks.

Therefore, if you are a beginner and have a good reason to be bearish about the overall market, begin with ETF puts before moving to trading puts on individual stocks. And as I've said before, don't even consider buying puts until you have practiced buying calls.

There is an old Wall Street saying that "puts are your friend." In fact, I have found, puts are not your friend. In reality, puts are like deceitful acquaintances who double-cross you at the first opportunity.

Here are a few observations about buying puts on individual stocks.

Trading Hint #1

It is not recommended that you buy puts on popular but overbought stocks. Darling stocks that are overbought can get more overbought. I have seen some very brilliant traders lose large sums of money by betting against popular stocks whose uptrend never seems to end.

One of the most notable examples is Tesla (TSLA), one of the most shorted stocks in the market at one time. The stock was both hated and loved. The heavy short positions had nothing to do with the worth of the company.

Many technical analysts saw that Tesla was overbought according to their indicators and shorted the shares. Nevertheless, that didn't prevent Tesla from rising even higher over several years, damaging the portfolios of short sellers and put owners who failed to cut their losses. Although Tesla plunged on some days, it almost always bounced back stronger than ever.

If you plan to buy puts on stocks, buy puts on weak, overbought stocks. When buying puts, never bet against the trend no matter what your indicators say, or what you "think."

Trading Hint #2

Puts are most useful when used as a hedge. This is how the pros use puts, and as you learn more about options, you can devise more sophisticated strategies (i.e., spreads). You can also use puts to protect existing stock portfolios or to hedge against market downturns.

· · · · · · · ·

Now that we talked about how to buy ETF calls and puts, it's time to move to Chapter 8, where you will learn some new strategies as well as read about a few old favorites.

Some of these strategies are for intermediate traders who have at least one year's trading experience. Because some involve a bit more risk, I refer them to the "off-the-wall" option strategies. Use them at your own risk!

8

Off-the-Wall Option Strategies

In this chapter, you will learn a number of options strategies, some of which involve increased risk. Here is a list of topics to be covered:

- The Long Shot
- Countertrend Strategies
- Basic Hedge Strategies
- The Simple One-Stock Strategy

The following strategies are different from the more stable strategies introduced earlier. Until now, I've shown you how to trade responsibly and patiently, and not take unnecessary risks.

There are times, however, when you may want to increase risk. If that is something of interest, you've come to the right place. There is nothing wrong with taking risks when trading options, as long as you follow our number one rule: Trade small, which means to not buy more contracts than you can afford.

Once again, you might want to read about these options strategies slowly, taking frequent breaks, rather than trying to understand everything at once.

Long Shot Strategy

I am almost reluctant to discuss this trade because it's more akin to gambling than trading, what I refer to as the Long Shot Strategy. If done properly, the amount of money you invest is low, but the payoff can be big (when you are right).

The key is not to risk too much money on a long shot, and more importantly, don't make this trade very often. Be warned that the following strategy is similar to buying a lottery ticket. Perhaps that's why it's so popular with so many options traders.

Here is the trade: Buy a deep out-of-the-money call or put with a long expiration date, perhaps two to three months.

For example, if SPY were at 300 and you were bearish, you would buy one or two puts at a strike price of 225 to 250 with a two- to three-month expiration date. Because the put is so deep out of the money, the cost of the option is cheap, no more than $3 to $4 per contract, and sometimes even less.

Because this trade is such a huge gamble, the chances are good that you will lose the entire investment. But that is the rationale for investing only a small sum, approximately $300 or $400 per trade.

I repeat: This is not a trade to make often, and typically, buy only a few contracts. If by some chance SPY plunged, the payoff would be large—thousands of dollars. Remember that SPY does not have to hit the strike price for you to earn a big payoff. Even if SPY dropped to $275 per share, the option profits would be substantial (depending on when the decline occurred). Nevertheless, this trade is a long shot.

Unfortunately, many options traders try these long shot trades on a regular basis and lose. They are similar to making a hole in one in golf, or betting on a long shot at a horse race—possible, but not probable.

Bottom line: There is nothing wrong with making infrequent, small-money bets on a long shot (with calls or puts). For the most part, stick with the trades mentioned in this book that involve less risk and offer better chances of success.

Countertrend Strategies

Countertrend Strategies—going against the trend—can succeed if your timing is impeccable. Although many books, including this one, recommend following the trend, sometimes the best trading profits come from doing the opposite of everyone else.

Be aware that many people who have never used countertrend strategies believe that "no one can time the market." In fact, some people *can* time the market, but no one said it was easy. Just because not everyone can time the market doesn't mean it can't be done. Most market timers use technical analysis to determine when to enter or exit a position, and you can, too.

There are also times when trend trading and momentum trading strategies do not work. For example, if a bull market slows down and eventually turns into a bear market, rallies will not last long, and, worse, are likely to reverse direction. That is when countertrend strategies shine.

The two most popular countertrend strategies are the Spike Up and the Spike Down, which were discussed in Chapter 6. Now I'll give ideas of how to trade them.

Countertrend Strategy: Spike Up

As you remember, a stock or index that spikes up (a nontechnical term that I defined) means the underlying stock moves up so fast and so high that it displays a vertical line on a chart. A Spike Up can occur at any time during the day, but it is during the opening when a countertrend strategy is most effective.

A Spike Up often appears first in the premarket, so when the major stock exchanges open, the spike is not a big surprise. When SPY and QQQ spike higher at the open, many times they will be unable to sustain the upward momentum and will stall. Inexperienced momentum traders will attempt to chase stocks or indexes that spike up, hoping the upward momentum will continue.

Many times the momentum not only stalls but reverses direction. As mentioned earlier, this is referred to as a *bull trap*, when the bulls believe the stock or index will keep rising, but instead it reverses direction. The bulls get trapped in the position and can't get out without a loss.

If you do detect a stock or index that is spiking up, betting against the trend can be profitable. Instead of chasing the stock or index higher, like momentum traders do, consider trading in the opposite direction by making a countertrend trade. No one said it was easy, so trade small if you attempt this trade!

Figure 8.1 shows a screenshot of a stock spiking higher, stalling, and reversing direction.

Here are a few observations:

1. If you use countertrend strategies, take the profits quickly, often within minutes. The profits may not last long.
2. *Warning*: This is a risky trade. Don't use this strategy on popular but overbought stocks. Beloved stocks that are overbought can get more overbought.

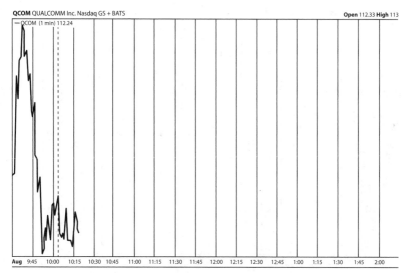

FIGURE 8.1 Stock spiking higher and reversing
Source: Chart courtesy of StockCharts.com

Countertrend Strategy: Spike Down

As you recall, a stock or index that spikes down means the stock or index falls so hard and so fast that you can see a vertical downtrend on a chart. Once again, although a Spike Down can appear at any time, it's most obvious when it occurs after the open.

More than likely, in the premarket, the indexes were already plunging. A stock or index that spikes down after the open may reverse direction as the crowd enters the market to buy on the dip at lower prices.

Again, this is a *bear trap*, which occurs when bears are holding profitable puts or short positions that suddenly reverse direction (Figure 8.2). This traps the bears in their short positions while the market is rising. All they can do is watch in horror as their profits disappear, or take immediate action to salvage some of their profit.

Figure 8.2 shows a one-minute chart of the Spike Down Reversal.

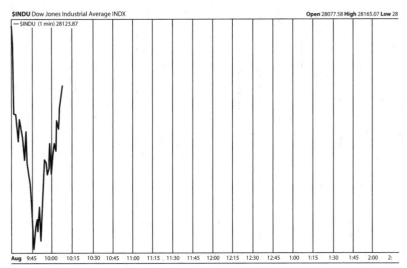

FIGURE 8.2 The Dow Jones Industrial Average (DJIA) spiking down and
suddenly reversing
Source: Chart courtesy of StockCharts.com

Here are a few observations:

1. There is an old but wise saying, "Never try to catch a falling
   knife." If a stock or index is plunging, it is not easy to buy
   at the low because it often keeps moving lower. Therefore,
   be sure to take any profits quickly (within minutes if using
   this strategy), as it's possible the market will fall again later.
   These are not easy trades to make.
2. This is a risky trade. If you buy calls on SPY or a falling stock
   and are proved wrong, your losses will multiply quickly.

Basic Hedge Strategies

Hedge strategies are fascinating, and they can range from simple to
complex. In fact, if I had to discuss all of the hedging strategies, I'd

have to write another book. Option hedge strategies include credit and debit spreads, straddles, and protective puts, to name a few. Many have sexy names such as the Iron Condor or the Butterfly. All these strategies are included in the second edition of my book *Understanding Options*.

Because complex hedge strategies are beyond the scope of this book, I am going to discuss only one such strategy. As you know, I don't think you should make complex trades until you have made a lot of practice trades first.

The simple hedge strategy below is one that I have tested and researched. There are several ways to use hedges. A hedge, by definition, is a risk-reducing strategy. However, you can also use hedges to make money. Let's discuss one method that aims to generate profits.

The High-Volatility Straddle

As I've said before, I urge traders to seldom hold option positions over a weekend (if you follow the strategies in this book). But there is one time when you may break that rule.

If you believe that the underlying stock will soon be making a big move, but you have no idea in which direction (up or down), you may want to consider buying a straddle. I call it a High-Volatility Straddle to help you remember that the best time to initiate a straddle is when you believe that volatility is going to move higher in the near future.

For example, before a major news event or earnings report, it is appropriate to buy a straddle. Any of these events can move the market or your stock, and you don't know in which direction. Basically, you are speculating that the price change of the options will be large enough for the position to earn a profit.

Therefore, you buy a *straddle*, which allows you to simultaneously own a bullish and bearish position (call and put). The higher the implied volatility of the underlying stock's options, the more you must pay to own the position. Why is implied volatility high?

Probably because market participants have a greater than normal expectation that the move will be big.

Unfortunately, if you buy the straddle when expectations are already high, you run the risk that implied volatility will collapse once the news is out. If the stock price did not undergo much of a change, you would lose money on both the call and the put.

The appeal of the straddle is that there is a chance, although small, that you can make money on both sides. That can occur when the news is so unexpected that implied volatility increases even further. Typically, that does not happen.

Therefore, to make a profit, the underlying stock must make a major move. Sometimes that doesn't happen and you lose money. You must test-trade this many times to get a feel of how option pricing behaves in these situations. Keep good records so that you can make comparisons.

As you will see, hedging with a straddle is a strategy you can use on rare occasions. It's common to lose money on each leg when implied volatility declines and the anticipated event fails to result in a significant price change.

The Simple One-Stock Strategy

The following is not an off-the-wall strategy, but it has worked well during bull markets. The Simple One-Stock Strategy is this: Buy options or buy stock in a popular stock that is in a strong uptrend, owned by many including Wall Street traders and most individual investors. In the past these favorites included Apple, Amazon, Microsoft, Alphabet, and Netflix, and in the future, there will be others, and many trading at much lower prices.

After choosing a stock with great potential, buy calls on it, using the strategies described in this book. In the right market environment, you can make very good money.

A Tale of Two Traders

I have two trader friends. Trader #1 is a professional trader with decades of experience. He's an expert in technical analysis and has dozens of indicators and oscillators on multiple charts with multiple time frames.

He uses technical analysis to identify the most overbought stocks, often technology stocks, and sells them short or buys puts on them. He also buys stable, low-priced stocks that are oversold.

After four years, my professional trader friend made small gains using his countertrend strategies. He was right more than 50 percent of the time, but when he was wrong, the losses damaged his account. A failure to follow his rules combined with a difficult strategy led to losses. Fortunately, he was an expert in risk management so he never lost a fortune when he was wrong. He never made much, either.

My other friend, Trader #2, is an amateur. He began by experimenting with debit and credit spreads, but he often got confused and abandoned the strategy.

He knows little about technical analysis, but he paid close attention to the fundamentals, and to any news about the companies whose stock and options he was trading. That's when he decided to focus on only one stock, Amazon. Using some of the strategies in this book, he bought calls on Amazon when the stock was $370 per share, a price that seemed high at the time.

My friend bought at-the-money calls with a two-month expiration date, and he held the calls until two weeks before expiration, when he sold the position. He repeated this strategy for four years. On occasion, he lost money, but he sold immediately when he detected any weakness. Because he chose the right stock at the right time, he got rich from owning calls on only one stock. Fortunately for him, Amazon bounced back after every sell-off.

In hindsight, Amazon's stock price was low at the time he bought, but no one knew just how low it was until Amazon went as high as $3,500 per share. "Low" and "high" are relative, and you never know until later the true value of any stock.

In other words, picking certain stocks in a bullish market environment, and holding for short or long time periods, can earn substantial profits. Finding the right stock is the key, but my friend also had to force himself not to get distracted by the hundreds of other stocks that seemed like better deals at the time. My friend focused only on one stock and ignored all the others. It paid off big time for him.

The Simple One-Stock Strategy works when the market environment or stock is in a strong uptrend. If you are reading this during a vicious bear market or correction, you must patiently wait until it ends. Then look for strong stocks with the most potential, and get ready to buy. It takes discipline to trade options on only one stock, but if you choose wisely, it can be extremely rewarding. These stocks are out there, but you have to do your research to find them.

The main point is that you do not need to use complicated strategies to make money in the market. If you can pick just one stock, and make it a good one, you can do well buying options or stocks.

And that is the Simple One-Stock Strategy that has made some people a lot of money in certain market environments. I am not a fan of buying and holding indefinitely, but if you use time stops and other risk-reducing strategies, you can make money buying calls on only one stock at a time.

· · · · · · · ·

By now, I'm assuming you have a lot of questions about what you've read so far. If you do, then the next chapter should meet your needs.

Based on inquiries I've received from readers, the next chapter includes a list of questions and answers about the Test Trading Strategy and trading tactics. Feel free to skip around and read the questions that are most important to you.

9

Questions and Answers

This chapter is for anyone who still has questions about the Test Trading Strategy. If you've been using the strategy for a while, it may seem like a review. If you're still unsure how it works, however, this chapter should help. Questions about trading tactics are also answered.

Questions About the Test Trading Strategy

Here are answers to questions I've received on the Test Trading Strategy. Choose to read the ones that interest you.

QUESTION: *Why should I set up test trades before the market opens? Why can't I make the test trades after the market opens?*
If you want to set up test trades after the market opens, you can. The reason to set up the trades prior to the opening is to save time. If you enter trades after the market opens, it takes time to enter a dozen or so stock orders.

It's really a personal choice for when to place a paper money order to buy. The point is that you are using the test trades to find winning stocks. That is the main goal. It makes no difference when you enter the paper money trades, as long as it's before or soon after the market opens.

QUESTION: *How much time do I need to set up the test trading account each day?*

There is no single correct answer because everyone works at a different pace. If you are new to trading options, or have not yet made your first trade, it may take as long as 15 minutes to make paper money trades on 100 to 500 shares of stock. It's also challenging at first to find winning stocks right after the market opens.

After the test trading account is set up properly, you will find that it takes less and less time to initiate positions in the account. On some days, it will take just a few minutes. On other days, when the market is ready to skyrocket higher, it may require 10 minutes to add all the stocks that are ready to open higher by at least 1 point (or 1 percent).

The more you practice, the better you will get at making trades. It may not be as much fun as trading with real money, but the trader who spends time practice-trading is going to fare better than the trader who doesn't.

The main idea is this: Every day that you make paper money trades in the test trading account is a day you learn something new. In my opinion, there is no downside to using simulated trading programs to find winning stocks or to improve your trading skills.

As Mr. Miyagi said in the great movie *The Karate Kid*, "Wax on . . . wax off." If you didn't see the movie, the advice is that doing mundane tasks such as applying wax on and off a car again and again can eventually lead you to learn karate, or to trade options.

QUESTION: *What if I don't have enough time to set up the test trading account before the market opens?*

You may be thinking that this daily routine will take a lot of time to set up each day, and you may not have the time. That is understandable. It's a problem for many people getting the test trading account ready for the market opening. Some traders have other jobs, or they might have errands to run or a dog to walk. Spending even 10 minutes setting up the account before the market opens will be difficult.

If you are unable to prepare test positions for that day, there are several choices. First, you can choose not to trade that day until you have more time. There is nothing wrong with taking days off from the trading business.

If you don't have the time to enter your test orders in the premarket, you can add them after the market opens. If the market is zooming higher in the premarket, the odds are good you will be able to find a winning stock or two that will move higher all day (although there are no guarantees since every trading day is different).

QUESTION: *Can you tell me how to quantify which stocks are true winners?*

This is an important question, but it's difficult to answer. There is no specific way to quantify which stocks are true winners except to watch what I call the "profit trend." If the profits in one stock are rapidly increasing, and you see "profit upticks," then that is a position you want to probe with five paper calls and then five more.

After buying five calls, watch the position closely. You may have at least a half dozen or more other stocks that are also moving higher. Try and identify the true winners.

If the paper money profits keep ticking higher and the overall market is moving in the right direction, the odds are good that the option position will move higher. If the profits keep rising and the stock is in an uptrend, you probably have a true winner, but in the trading world, nothing is certain.

So when do you stop watching and get on board? That is the part that is hard to quantify. By watching closely, you should find stocks that are on the move. Look at a chart to confirm the underlying stock is trending higher. Unfortunately, sometimes you might pick a stock that goes nowhere.

Eventually, you will find a champion that emerges from the pack, and that is the one you want to buy. Be patient until you find the true winner, and once you do, buy it in the real brokerage account.

I must be honest with you: Identifying a true winner is not always clear-cut. Even when profits are ticking in the right direction, there could be a sudden reversal. When the overall market is on your side, it's much easier to trade.

In addition, some stocks are more volatile and, thus, unpredictable. It's ideal if you are watching a Steady Eddie stock, but often the wildest, most volatile stocks turn out to be the biggest winners. When using this strategy, or any other, it's important that you first learn how to manage risk in case you are wrong.

With training and also studying the market each day, you will get better and better at picking out true winners. Don't expect to be an expert in only a few days. Give yourself time. Also, if you are reading this book during a bull market, it will be easier to find stocks that bring you the most profits. In a bear market or correction, you will have to work harder for your money.

> *Bottom line:* It is difficult to quantify when is the right time to buy, but once you see that a stock or ETF is steadily moving in the right direction with the power of the stock market behind it, the odds are very good you have identified a winner.

QUESTION: *When is the best time to buy an option when using the Test Trading Strategy?*
I've discussed this earlier, but it's so important I'm going to address it further.

The most difficult part of using any strategy, including the Test Trading Strategy, is deciding when to buy. As a trader, the entry point is one of the most important decisions you ever make, and unfortunately, many traders do not give it much thought.

Perhaps I have convinced you to be more careful than other traders by making extra tests. The downside of all this checking is that you are probably going to miss out on some profitable opportunities. That is the price of being cautious. We want to minimize risk while seeking gains. I'd rather lose potential profits than lose real money.

Obviously, you can confirm your trade decisions with technical analysis, although it's not required. No matter what method you use, the main point is that you must get the entry right. Of course you will make mistakes by entering at the wrong time, or being careless. It happens. But the more you trade, the more experience you gain. Hopefully, over time you will learn how to buy the right stocks at the right time.

Is it easy? No! Every day there is a new winning stock and a new trading environment. Just when you think you have some of the answers, that's when the market confuses and deceives you, costing money.

However, if you entered at a fairly good price, even when wrong, the losses usually won't be severe. It's when you enter at the wrong time and at the wrong price that you can lose big. Again, and I hate to keep repeating, if you test before you trade, you let the test trading program do the probe for you, which costs you nothing. Then you can decide whether to enter at that time or wait.

Note: Speaking of time, you will typically try to find a winning stock within the first hour, and if you can't find one, you can stop trading for the rest of the day (with few exceptions).

QUESTION: *Why do you only buy calls when setting up the test trading account? I like to buy puts.*

This is a good question. Obviously, there is nothing to prevent you from setting up a short position on certain days. Based on my research, however, I have found it is less risky to trade the long side each day.

On the other hand, on the days when the overall market is due to plummet, and it's difficult to find any stocks to buy, it may be time to get short by buying puts. I've found that when the market is weak and falling, it is easier to buy SPY and QQQ puts rather than individual stocks. However, that may change in the future if we enter into a lengthy bear market.

In addition, every trader has a different way of seeing things, so it's a personal choice. Those who are comfortable buying puts on weak individual stocks can do so. I admittedly still need to do more research using the test trading account on put buying. Nevertheless, those who are ready to buy puts should do so by first using technical analysis to identify a proper entry or exit.

QUESTION: *What happens if I get conflicting signals in the test trading account? Should I trade that day?*

This is also a good question because it happens often. Sometimes you get divergent signals; i.e., SPX (or SPY) might be falling while the Dow is rising. On other occasions, the chart shows the market is moving in one direction while individual stocks do the opposite. Divergent signals are a warning sign, and to play it safe, trade lightly or not at all until the conflict is resolved.

Eventually, the market resolves the conflict when one direction or the other dominates. However, it may not happen until the next day. Most importantly, it's wise to avoid trading when the signals and trend are unclear. Don't attempt to eke out a profit on these days. Be patient.

QUESTION: *How do you identify a dangerous market?*
As mentioned previously, a divergence is a warning sign. Perhaps the market is not as strong (or as weak) as it appears, and a reversal is imminent.

After you spend time studying the stock market every day, you will get better at recognizing risky market environments. When you do, be disciplined enough to avoid trading. Just like a pilot won't fly when poor weather looms, wise traders avoid putting money in the market when conditions are unfavorable.

As you gain expertise as a market observer and student of the market, you will recognize dangerous (high-risk) stock market behavior patterns such as the Sideways Sucker and Rocky Road. When you see these patterns on the chart, you will know not to trade those stocks at that time.

Most important, don't feel compelled to trade every day. When you detect unpredictable or dangerous market conditions, avoid trading.

QUESTION: *My friends are professional traders who say that simulated trading programs are unrealistic and don't work. What should I tell them?*
If you mention the word *testing*, many pros will believe you are referring to backtesting, a complex and somewhat controversial method of evaluating strategies by using data from the past. Explain that you are not backtesting.

Nevertheless, many pros are not fans of using a paper money account. They believe it's useless and offers misleading results. For example, they assume that you will pretend to buy an unrealistic number of contracts such as 50 or 100 contracts. You won't do that, but the pros think you will.

The other complaint is that if you use a simulated program, you won't feel the pain of losing real money. That's true. In this book, however, the primary purpose of the paper money account is not to simulate trades, but to find winning stocks as well as provide clues to market direction. This will be difficult for professional traders to believe.

Therefore, expect to be misunderstood when you discuss any of the test trading strategies in this book. The ideas are so new that no one will know what you are talking about. The pros will also be suspicious of new strategies they never heard of.

What should you tell them? Not much. But listen to your professional friends, as they may have useful information about technical analysis that can give clues to market direction.

QUESTION: *My professional trader friend says that I am chasing after momentum stocks, which he says is a high-risk strategy. Is he right?*
You will get that criticism from anyone who doesn't understand trend trading. If you use the strategies in this book, you will be trading from a list of approximately 80 stocks, including some of the most well-known and popular stocks in the world. On many days, one or more of these stocks will explode higher.

On some days, certain stocks on your Watch List might zoom higher by 7 or 8 percent at the open. Do not chase these stocks. Instead, track their upward momentum. On especially good days, they might start the morning up only 1 or 2 percent and end up as high as 4 or 5 percent. These are the stocks that can bring the most profits.

Are you using a momentum strategy? I'd call it a trend trading momentum strategy. Just because there is strong momentum pushing the stocks higher is no reason to decline to trade it.

One difference between momentum trading and the methods you are learning is this: Instead of chasing after stocks that are rising quickly, by using the strategies you learned in this book, you will test before you trade. Regular Momo (momentum) traders don't test first; they just chase. They would not test first because it takes too much time for them.

> *Bottom line:* Don't argue with other traders who insist that their strategies are best. Everyone thinks his or her strategy is best! Just use strategies that work for you regardless of what they are called. Don't be like your myopic friend who refuses to learn new strategies, new tools, or new ideas.

QUESTION: *Should I buy a stock with a bad reputation even if it is going up in the test trading account?*

Unlike the stocks in your Watch List, on occasion you might want to trade a stock with a "bad boy" reputation, the kind of stock favored by day traders and scalpers. These high-risk candidates appear often on our buy lists, and they are worth monitoring.

One year precious metals were extremely volatile, another year it was marijuana stocks, and some years certain technology stocks were risky. Some of these stocks may be on your Watch List. In my opinion, any stock is in play as long as it has not spiked higher.

To answer your question, yes, you can buy stocks that are volatile, but trade small and take profits fast. So if a hot stock appears on your test trading screen, feel free to test and follow it.

Once you decide to buy it in the real brokerage account, put less money at risk. For example, even one contract on an expensive high-flying stock can cost big bucks, as Sam found out when he bought Tesla options. If the risk is too great, just pass on the trade. In addition, think of the worst-case scenario—how much you could lose. Then proceed with caution.

Personally, I would not hold one of the wild stocks overnight, but that is a decision only you can make. On occasion the Momo stocks keep moving higher for days and weeks, which could result in a tidy little return. My advice: Sell by Friday no matter what happens.

QUESTION: *Often, I see one or more stocks that keep moving higher all morning. Should I buy this stock after it's made a big move?*

Most of the time, the answer is no. The key to success in using the Test Trading Strategy is getting in early and then selling for a decent profit later in the day. If you do miss out on a really good trade, don't beat yourself up or get frustrated. Every day, there are other potential winning stocks. It's always better to miss an opportunity than to lose money from being late.

QUESTION: *At what point should you make a real trade after identifying a winning stock?*

This is an important question but without an easy answer. There is no specific time or amount of profit that triggers a buy signal. Unfortunately, trading is often more art than science.

With practice, and after making dozens of test trades, you will have a better feel for when it's time to buy. You won't always be right, but you will learn to evaluate when the odds are on your side, including which stocks have a tendency to disappoint.

When profits in the test trading account are upticking, it may be time to buy for real. You should also check the chart for both the individual stock and overall market. When you put all the clues together and it looks good, you can go ahead and place an order to buy. If you're still not sure, make another test purchase, or wait a little longer for further verification.

If you bought at the right time and at the right price, you should earn a profit. The stock and option positions should be watched closely. If you were wrong in your analysis, and the position is losing money, use a time stop and a stop loss (based on how much money you are prepared to lose) to manage risk.

If the position continues to lose money, consider selling even within minutes if you decide that the entry was poor. However, if the position is making money, be prepared to follow your trade plan that included when to sell (hopefully you set a profit target before buying). If you chose a profitable stock, the gains may keep increasing. Nevertheless, watch the position closely until you decide to exit.

QUESTION: *Why do you let so many trades go? Doesn't that make you frustrated that you keep missing so many good trades?*
One of the requirements for being a disciplined trader is keeping your emotions under control. And that means not getting greedy or panicked. Greed is especially difficult to manage because it results in overtrading, taking too much risk, and chasing every stock that is moving.

To be a disciplined trader, you must accept that there are limits to how many positions you can own at one time. You also cannot expect to make money on every trade. In fact, with the Test Trading Strategy, you are focused on only one or two positions, and that means letting potential winners, and potentially profitable opportunities, go.

Train yourself not to worry or care about all the money you "could have" made with other stocks. Concentrate on managing the position that you own. There will be times when you'll miss an option that "would have" given you a huge gain if you had held another week, or even a month. Everyone has a could-have, would-have, should-have story, and although annoying, you must follow your rules and focus on your current trades.

There is one trading situation that not only is annoying, but will cause you the most psychological damage. That is when you made big profits, and it shows in your trading account balance, but you neglected (for whatever reason) to sell. This takes an emotional toll, and it is one of the reasons for taking profits, and not getting greedy and selling too late.

I've seen traders, including myself, make $20,000, $100,000, $300,000, and in one case, $1 million (one of my friends), who did not take their profits when they had the chance. In all cases, the profits disappeared. For almost every trader, a huge profit can be a life-changing event, and it is just plain foolish to let it get away. Losing money that was in your account is much more painful than losing money you "could" have had.

> *Bottom line:* Don't worry about the imaginary profits you could have made. Instead, focus on the real profits that are in your trading account right now.

QUESTION: *What if I am losing money using your strategy?*
Not everyone will take the time to learn and fully understand a new trading strategy. The Test Trading Strategy takes a little time to set up every morning before the market opens. If you have followed the instructions in this book and are still unable to make money, do not get upset.

As mentioned before, you can also use technical analysis, which might work out better for you. In addition, if trading is not your passion, you can always adopt the traditional strategy of investing, not trading. For most people, investing is their primary strategy, and trading is secondary.

No matter what strategy you use, try to evaluate why you are losing money. Is it because the strategy is poorly designed, or the indicators are unreliable, or you are making too many mistakes? Very few people were born to be traders. It is a skill that can take years to learn, and in fact, most people lose money when they are first starting out. That is another reason why it's better to lose money in a virtual account than in a real-money account.

> *Most important:* Not everyone can make money trading, just like not everyone can be an airplane pilot or a writer or a musician. At some point, if you are not making money trading using the strategies in this book or other strategies, it is perfectly acceptable to stop trading.

If you can't make money as a trader, don't take it personally. Find other ways to increase your income. Consider investing in a mutual fund or index fund. You can also hire someone else to manage your account. It's essential that you know yourself, including your strengths and weaknesses. Don't try to force yourself to be a trader if you have neither the motivation nor the skills to succeed.

QUESTION: *What if there is a bear market? Will the strategies in this book still work?*
I'm glad you asked, because you could be reading this during a bear market. It's true that the strategies in this book are mostly aimed at going long the stock market (buying calls). Even during a vicious bear market, there are strong "knock-your-socks-off" rallies (the so-called *bear market rally*). The Test Trading Strategy should work on the days the rally occurs. And even when bear market rallies last longer than a few days, you can still use the Test Trading Strategy.

However, if a lengthy, vicious bear market occurs, you have several choices:

1. Buy QQQ and SPY puts on the days when technical indicators point to a lower market, also confirmed by a lack of winners in the test trading account.
2. Do not sell stocks short because the risk of large losses is too great. *Warning:* I do not recommend selling short stocks in the real trading account. If you want to bet against the market, buy puts.
3. Follow the trend: Buy calls on stocks when there is an uptrend. Buy puts on stocks when there is a downtrend.

One of the main points is that when the market environment changes and the overall trend also changes, you must be flexible enough to change with it. Some of the worst losses I have ever witnessed come from traders who were unwilling to change with the market.

Traders who insist on betting against a bull market with puts have incurred the largest losses. And in a bear market, as the market continuously falls, those who insist on buying every dip will generate losses.

It's a simple idea, but to make money in the market, follow the trend. Fighting the market not only is difficult but usually ends in disaster. To help you remember, to the tune of the classic song "I Fought the Law" (and the law won), remember these words: I fought the market and the market won.

> *Bottom line:* In the end, the market always wins. It may not be fair, it may not be right, but the market always wins, because the market is always right. It is the only opinion that counts. In addition, the market is never static, and you can't be either. Keep testing and experimenting until you find what works no matter what the market environment.

QUESTION: *Do winners only break out and emerge in the morning?*

With the Test Trading Strategy, most of the time the winning stocks can be found soon after the open. That is when you have the best chance of finding an early winner that will continue all morning, and hopefully all day.

However, during the day, some stocks can suddenly emerge as winners. It is a personal choice whether you want to buy these latecomers. Most traders have their hands full with the early winners. There often isn't enough time to follow late winners. It's really a personal choice whether you want to look for potential winners all day.

You may find, as I did, that the biggest profits occur if you catch winning stocks early, usually within the first hour. If you catch a successful stock later in the day, although profits can be made, it can be a little more challenging unless the market builds up strength in the afternoon. This is definitely possible on some days.

Bottom line: It's your decision whether to trade early or late, but winning stocks can break out at any time of the day.

QUESTION: *You sometimes say to wait and see. How long should I wait before I pull the trigger and make a trade?*
If you were using technical analysis, you would use indicators and oscillators to help with timing the buy and sell decisions. That's what most traders use. However, if you are using the Test Trading Strategy, your main signal to buy occurs when profits increase to a predetermined sum, an amount that you specify. That's why you often have to "wait and see."

In addition, because you are also using a time stop, your trades will almost always occur prior to 11:00 a.m. ET (this is a general guideline, not a rule). Obviously, there are traders who continue to buy options all day. On most days, however, you should be able to find a winning stock rather quickly. Besides, if you are day-trading, you seldom want to open a new position in the afternoon.

So what are you waiting for? You are waiting for all the signals to line up correctly, and most importantly, for a winning stock to emerge from the stocks in the test trading account. When one or more of these stocks appear, and the overall market is on your side, you can make a trade.

QUESTION: *I am confused by your strategy. Why not buy low and sell high?*
One trader I know told me: "I have been trained to buy low and sell high. I was also taught that the only way to make money with options was buying when implied volatility is low, and before the stock already moved higher. You are suggesting buying options on stocks that already moved higher and as implied volatility rises. I think I missed the boat on this trade."

This is my answer: By all means, buy low and sell high if you have the skills to know when it is time to buy. The Test Trading Strategy is not for everyone, but it does increase the chances of owning a winning position.

For many beginners, technical analysis is confusing and difficult to understand, or even worse, they use it before knowing what they are really doing. The Test Trading Strategy is an alternative method for identifying winning stocks. It's your choice whether to use both methods or only one.

This strategy may not work for you, so don't feel obligated to use it just because you are reading this book. If you already use technical analysis (or another method) to find potential winners, keep using what works for you. The Test Trading Strategy is designed for novice traders who may be intimidated or confused by technical analysis. It is easy to set up and use, as long as you have access to a simulated trading account.

Predicting which stocks will move higher is a popular strategy that is often unprofitable, but many make the attempt every day. As option traders, if you are wrong about the market direction, you will lose money, and quickly. Rather than guessing which stocks will move higher, the Test Trading Strategy encourages you to follow stocks in an uptrend.

You are correct that you could be overpaying for implied volatility. And you are also not getting a good deal on your option purchases with this strategy because you may be paying a lofty premium. However, when selling the same day, you are very likely to sell the position at the same lofty implied volatility. In other words, it's a wash.

If you don't like the idea of buying popular momentum stocks, or following trending stocks, then don't have those stocks on your Watch List.

Finally, instead of being so quick to criticize the strategy, why don't you take the time and give it a try? On days when certain stocks are on the move and trending higher, if you "ride the wave" and buy into the uptrend, you may be surprised at the money you can make, even though you may be overpaying for the options.

In theory, we all want to buy low and sell high, but in real life that is extremely difficult to do unless you are a superb market timer. Therefore, instead of trying to predict which stocks will be winners, use the Test Trading Strategy to find the winners.

I'm not saying this options strategy is for everyone, and it may not be for you. If you have a strategy that is already working, then use it. There is plenty of other useful information in the book you can read besides the Test Trading Strategy.

Questions About Trading Tactics

Here are answers to questions on trading tactics. I hope you find them helpful.

QUESTION: *Are you promoting day trading?*
I'm not promoting any strategy, including day trading. In this book, I introduce a variety of strategies, and it's up to you to decide which, if any, fits your personality and makes sense for you. Some people are comfortable buying and selling within the same day, while others do better by holding longer. There is no right answer, because everyone is different.

As most people know, day trading involves opening and closing a position on the same day. It's also true that we often buy and sell within one day, so we are day trading. However, we do not use traditional day-trading strategies that have you frantically buying and selling dozens of option positions for small profits.

Bottom line: I wouldn't be that concerned about the label as long as the strategy works for you.

QUESTION: *Could you elaborate on overnight trading? What do you mean by this?*

Overnight trading refers to holding an option position overnight. You can buy a call option near the end of the day and hold it overnight. You would do this if you believe the market, or an individual stock, will rise the next day.

You may remember that if you do make an overnight trade, it will typically be with a call. It is relatively rare that you will hold a put overnight, because the odds are likely to be against you—unless it is a bear market or correction.

When using the strategies described in this book, most of the time you will sell options when market prices are at extreme levels—that means near market high points when trading calls, or near market low points when trading puts—on the same day.

Overnight trading can be used on occasion, but not consistently. The reason is simple: No one can predict what will happen the next morning, and when trading options, when you're wrong, you can lose money just from holding until the next day. Nevertheless, holding calls overnight has worked during bullish market environments.

QUESTION: *What do you mean by weekly trading?*

Weekly trading refers to selling most (usually all) your option positions before the close of trading on Friday. Weekly trading is similar to *swing trading*, where a position is held for three to five days.

The main point is that you are not locked into any time frame. Most of the time, you should plan to exit option positions within the same day. But if you are on a winning streak with a given position, you may decide to hold for the rest of the week. That's flexibility.

> *Bottom line:* Get in the habit of selling option positions in a timely manner. Monday morning, you will have avoided all weekend worries and awaken refreshed and prepared for trading.

QUESTION: *Should I buy puts?*

After years of testing and experimenting with puts, I discovered that it's easier to buy calls than puts. If you plan to buy puts, however, it's often less risky to trade ETF puts such as SPY and QQQ rather than puts on individual stocks (not always, but often).

Puts are fantastic moneymakers when you catch a downtrend in its early stages. They also provide excellent trade opportunities during bear markets or corrections.

The problem with buying puts is that the financial world wants the market to move higher. That includes investors, financial institutions, the Fed, and almost everyone connected to Wall Street. Therefore, on many days when the market is falling, major financial entities and traders may enter the market with buy-on-the-dip orders. It doesn't always happen, but it happens enough so you should be on guard.

Obviously, there are professional traders with excellent timing skills who buy puts on stocks and earn excellent profits. But for the average retail investor betting against the financial interests of the big players, you should begin by buying ETF puts.

You can practice your put-buying skills on individual stocks later. I know traders who continuously (and stubbornly) bet against certain stocks that were in an uptrend just because the stocks were overbought. Guess what happened? The stocks kept going higher.

Stocks can remain overbought far longer than anyone thought possible. Therefore, it's often a mistake to bet against a stock or index just because it's overbought. Buying puts on individual stocks is a difficult game to play. And although the rewards can be fantastic when the timing is right, the risk is too great for most beginners. Puts are like hot potatoes: Hold them too long and you may get burned.

Hint: First master the long side of the market before thinking of buying puts on stocks.

QUESTION: *I had large gains in the morning, and now they disappeared. What should I do?*
Nothing can rob you of self-confidence more than losing money on a winning position. To minimize that from happening, keep close watch on your option position. After buying a short-term option, if you have substantial gains, always look for an opportunity to sell.

One selling guideline to think about: If a previously profitable option position falls to $0 or a little below, consider selling the entire position. You may have lost all previous gains, but at least you didn't lose money on the trade. There will be other opportunities to make money with other options, or another stock.

Some traders may believe that selling at the zero point is too strict. If you feel that way, you can always wait a little longer to see if the once profitable position bounces back. By the end of the day, however, if the option is still in the red, the wisest move is to sell the position and look for other opportunities.

> *Trading hint:* As a trader, you can't depend on luck or hope to make money. You must take action when a former winner turns into a loser.

QUESTION: *What do you mean by trading like a scientist?*
It means you have no feelings or attachment to the underlying stocks that you trade. It means being emotionless and unbiased, and focused only on the facts and not feelings or hunches. If you are using the strategies in this book, let the winning stocks prove themselves. You don't care which stock wins, only that you have identified it as a winner.

When you trade like a scientist, you don't take losses personally. Losses present an opportunity to gain knowledge. Also, just like a scientist, write down the mistakes you make and the lessons you learn in your trading notebook.

QUESTION: *How long should I hold a winning stock?*
Like so many questions, there is no right answer. Traders have used technical indicators as well as price targets to help determine when to buy or sell. Others have rules to help with the decision.

It's not easy to sell a winner. If you sell too early, you may miss additional gains after you sold. Many traders kick themselves and mumble, "I *should* have held it longer."

In this case, you made a decent profit, but if you had held longer, perhaps you could have made more money. As you recall, that's how Sam felt when he missed selling his option positions for a gain in Chapter 1. But once the options are sold, it no longer matters how the price changes.

On the other hand, if you hold a winning stock too long, profits may disappear. As mentioned earlier, letting a winning position turn into a loser is one of the most aggravating things that can happen to a trader. It is emotionally hurtful. At least when you sell a winner too early, you have some gains.

To solve this dilemma, when you have a big winner, instead of selling all, you could sell half now and prepare to sell the other half later. It is called "scaling out" of a position. This selling strategy works because it accomplishes two goals: locking in profits and reducing risk.

> *Bottom line:* It takes a lot of practice to know when to sell a winning position. But in general, take the profits while they are available, because gains from winning options have a way of disappearing before you are able to claim the winnings as your own.

QUESTION: *I own Netflix calls, and the stock is going to plunge by 10 percent when the market opens. I'm panicking. What should I do?*
This is an awful but common predicament, especially when holding options for too long. As I am writing this, I am watching the

stock of a great company, Netflix, fall by more than 10 percent in the after-hours market (due to comments from the CEO on future guidance). When the market opens in the morning, anyone holding a bullish Netflix position will suffer severe losses as the stock opens for trading.

If you own stock in Netflix, you can hold longer because the odds are excellent the stock will recover from this hiccup and have an excellent future. That's one of the advantages of holding stock: Time is on your side.

But if you own options, time is not on your side. In this case, there is nothing that you can do about the expiration date and deteriorating time value. This is a perfect example of why holding options increases risk. Although you can't lose more money than you invested, in this worst-case scenario, it's likely that you will lose a large chunk of your investment.

So what do you do? First, if you are holding a large losing position at the open, don't panic. Normally, you want to cut losers quickly, but if the loss occurs at the open, and if the option may be nearly worthless, wait a little while before selling.

It's possible the stock will reverse direction at some point during the day, or later in the week. Unfortunately, no one can guarantee it will recover quickly enough to help your investment.

If the stock does bounce back later in the week, you can take the opportunity to sell the calls for a small loss. However, if the stock keeps falling, it may be too late to salvage cash from the position.

Although you are feeling emotional right now, don't make any irrational moves. Today will not be a pleasant ordeal, but if you are patient, it's possible Netflix will recover in the near future. As for your calls retaining value, it depends on the strike price and how far away expiration is.

Bottom line: It's awful to get trapped in a losing position whether holding calls or puts. You want to cut your losses, but at the same time, you don't want to sell in a panic.

· · · · · · · · ·

Congratulations for taking the time to read and finish Part Three. I hope that you now know a lot more about how to find winning stocks using different options strategies and how to identify and react to stock market behavior.

In Part Four, I teach beginners (or experienced traders who need a refresher course) options basics, as well as provide an introduction to technical analysis.

In addition, in Part Four you will read about one of the greatest speculators in history, Jesse Livermore, and some of the trading tactics he used.

PART FOUR

THE BASICS

Part Four is designed to help the beginner options trader get up to speed with options vocabulary, as well as learn about the two most popular and useful technical indicators, moving averages and RSI (relative strength indicator).

It also includes a fascinating look at the life and trading tactics of the speculator Jesse Livermore, who was one of the first to use a trend-following strategy.

If you have never traded options before, or need a refresher course, Chapter 10 should be what you are looking for. If you already know the basics, feel free to skip to the next chapter.

However, if you are a beginner who has never opened an options account, you are in the right place. I will show you how to get started and introduce you to options basics.

10

Options Minicourse

This chapter is a little different because it is a minicourse, designed to help anyone with limited knowledge become familiar with options vocabulary and characteristics.

However, if you have the time and want to read an entire book on options, I recommend my bestselling book, *Understanding Options*, 2nd edition (McGraw-Hill). This book is for anyone who has little or no knowledge about trading options and is eager to learn about all the options strategies, from basic to advanced.

Now, let's learn about buying calls and puts.

Options Basics

If you have not yet traded options or need a quick review, this minicourse should meet your needs. The purpose of this chapter is to help you understand enough about options so that you can read and comprehend the contents of this book.

The focus of the minicourse is to help you become familiar with options vocabulary, as well as entering into your first trade. Before using the strategies in this book, or placing a real trade, it's essential to learn the basics. Consider the following information a crash course on trading options.

Opening an Options Trading Account

Before you begin, I suggest that you open an options trading account at a brokerage firm. It takes no more than 30 minutes to open an account, and you can do it online.

There are many brokerage firm choices, but choose a well-known firm with a lot of assets, fast trade executions, and easy-to-use trading screens. In addition, choose a broker with helpful representatives that you can talk with by either phone or chat. When trading options, there may be times when you have to communicate with a human.

It's best if the broker has a simulated trading program, but even if the broker doesn't have one, there are paper money programs online that you can use. In the future, more brokerage firms will offer simulated trading accounts as customers demand it.

When opening the account, let the representatives know that in addition to buying stocks, you also intend to buy and sell *calls* and *puts*, a so-called *Level 2 strategy*. Buying and selling calls and puts is the primary strategy we will be using in this book.

Why Should You Trade Options?

Options, one of the most fascinating financial instruments ever created, have many uses. Quite a few professional traders use options to protect stock portfolios, but they can also be used for speculation. In this book, we are primarily using options for speculation.

For example, one reason that many traders like options is that these traders can use them as leverage to earn many times their investment. To be more specific, for a small sum, options allow traders to control a lot more shares of stock than they can afford to buy.

Another big advantage of using options is that they come with limited risk. In other words, the options buyer knows the maximum possible loss on any trade. Options are especially popular with traders because they can be used as a hedging tool to reduce risk.

Unfortunately, options also have a reputation as a way to "get rich quick" because many traders have hit it big, while others have lost large sums. In this book, the focus will always be on managing risk so that losses are relatively small.

The Unique Vocabulary and Characteristics of Options

Now for the hard part. If you are new to trading options, the minicourse may seem like you are learning a new language, and you are. Options trading has its own language that will seem unusual, at least at first. Once you begin trading with the strategies described in this book, you will quickly get accustomed to the unique vocabulary words. Be patient and give yourself time to learn.

What Are Options?

All options are contracts that give you the right to buy something specific, like stock, but you are not required to do so. Although you have the right to buy stock (or ETFs), we are just going to trade the option contracts and will not actually buy the stock.

Because we are buying and selling option contracts and not trading stocks, the cost is a lot less than if we were buying stocks. That is another reason why options are so popular.

Now, I'm going to introduce you to the specialized language of options, which will help you understand them.

The Underlying Stock

An option contract (which is what we are buying) is just a paper contract that gives you the right to buy or sell something, such as stocks or ETFs. Therefore, every option contract is linked to a single stock, called an *underlying stock*. The option cannot exist unless it is attached to that underlying stock.

Not all stocks can have options. For example, penny stocks, or stocks that are less than $5 per share, usually are not allowed to have options. On the other hand, the most well-known and popular stocks, such as Apple, Alphabet, Netflix, Amazon, Walmart, and McDonald's, to name a few, all have their options listed on an exchange.

In this book, we will be buying and selling options on heavily traded stocks. That's where the money is, and trading those options will also give you more trading opportunities.

The Options Formula

There is one formula you must know before trading options: 1 option contract = 100 shares of stock. To clarify, 1 option contract gives you (the owner of the option) the "right" to buy 100 shares of stock. Therefore, if you bought or sold 1 option contract, that would be the same as if you had bought or sold 100 shares of stock. In this example, you control 100 shares of stock.

Another example: If you had bought or sold 5 contracts, that is equal to buying 500 shares of stock. In the options world, you use 100 as the multiplier when deciding how many options to buy or sell.

One common mistake that beginners make is confusing contracts with shares. So they may enter an order to trade 100 contracts instead of 1 contract. Do you know what that means? It means they attempted to buy the rights to 10,000 shares of the underlying stock! Of course, the brokerage firm would prevent the trade from proceeding unless there was enough money in the account.

Don't confuse contracts with shares: 1 contract = 100 shares of stock. In this book, you will almost always trade between 1 and 10 option contracts. Even under the most ideal conditions, you will probably not trade more than 20 option contracts (equal to 2,000 shares of stock). As mentioned earlier, another way to avoid getting into trouble trading options is by trading small, and that means owning between 1 and 10 option contracts.

Calls and Puts

There are two types of options, *calls* and *puts*. With these two options, you can only take two actions: buy or sell. In fact, although there are dozens of options strategies, ranging from simple to very complicated, they are all based on buying and selling calls and puts in various combinations.

Call

A *call* is a bullish position that is similar to "going long" a stock. Therefore, when you buy a call on a stock and the stock goes higher, the call increases in value. Conversely, if you are wrong and the stock goes lower, you will lose money (because the value of the call loses money).

The brilliant part about buying options is that you can participate in the upswing of a stock without actually owning the shares, and for a lot less money. Most of the strategies you will learn here will be focused on buying calls on individual stocks or ETFs (exchange-traded funds).

Put

A *put* is a bearish position that is similar to shorting a stock. Therefore, when you buy a put on a stock and the stock goes lower, the put will increase in value, and you make money. Conversely, if you are wrong and the stock goes higher, you will lose money.

The wonderful part about buying puts is that in certain market environments such as when the market is plunging, owning puts will be very profitable. Unfortunately, as you will learn as you keep reading, it is often more challenging to make money buying puts.

That is true because the entire financial world is geared to betting that stocks and the economy will keep going higher. Therefore, most of the strategies in this book are aimed at buying calls, not puts, but it's important that you learn how to buy both.

One fact you should not forget: Buying puts is a lot less risky than *shorting stocks*. I do not recommend that a new trader sell stocks short. If you buy puts on a stock and are wrong, the most you can lose is the cost of the puts. That's bad enough. But if you short a stock and you are wrong, you can lose a theoretically unlimited amount.

The Secret of Options

When the underlying stock or index goes up in price, the call option usually follows in the same direction. In other words, if you pick an underlying stock whose price is rising, expect that your calls will go up in value. Therefore, when you believe the underlying stock will be moving higher, buy calls on it.

This is important because if an underlying stock moves higher, so do its calls. That is the secret to making money in options, and the heart of the strategies in this book.

Conversely, if you believe the underlying stock will be moving lower, buy puts on it. Therefore, if the underlying stock or index falls, then the put will go up in value.

Even more important, the secret to success is choosing the right underlying stock. Where the stock goes, the option almost always follows. This is how we earn profits using options. We buy call options on rising stocks and buy puts on declining stocks.

Therefore, if you can find a stock or index that is moving higher and you buy calls on it, you can make money. When you find a stock or index that is moving lower, buy puts on it.

I don't want you to think that it's going to be that easy, because it's not. Just know that finding the right stocks at the right time should be your number one goal.

The Strike Price

The *strike price* is the fixed price at which you can buy or sell the underlying stock. For example, if a stock is selling for $102 per share, and you want to buy calls on this stock, you have to select a strike price. The closer it is to the stock price, the better, with some exceptions.

A strike price is the price at which you are willing to buy 100 shares, and you have a choice of many different strike prices. For example, a stock like Apple might have strike prices from $5 all the way to $200 (and higher). The strike prices are generally available in 1-point, 5-point, or 10-point increments. In this book, we will usually choose strike prices that are in 1-point and 5-point increments, but that is a personal choice.

> *Note:* If you are new to trading options, this may seem confusing at first, but it will become clear as you make more practice trades.

Premium

If you are a buyer, the *premium* is the price that you pay for an option. If you are a seller, this is the price you receive. Just like in an auction, the premium constantly changes throughout the trading day. If you are familiar with the stock market, the premium is the current market price. It is the price you paid or received for the contract.

> *Hint:* The premium is listed in the options trading account as the current market price of the contract.

Expiration Date

Another unique characteristic of options is they always expire. After a certain date and time, called the *expiration date*, options turn into a worthless piece of electronic paper. It is important to remember that options lose value over time and eventually cease to exist.

Once you buy an option, the clock is ticking. That is what makes options risky. Unlike with stocks, which can be held indefinitely, option contracts always expire. It is essential that you are aware of this time limit.

Thus, when buying options, not only must you be right about the direction of the underlying stock, but the underlying stock must move in the right direction before the option expires. Traders have lost a great deal of money by holding onto their options far longer than necessary. You are not going to fall into that trap.

The expiration date is part of every option contract. The most heavily traded options expire on the third Friday of each month at 4:00 p.m. ET. When expiration arrives, if the underlying stock did not perform as expected, the option will expire worthless (with very few exceptions).

In addition to the monthly expiration dates, weekly options are also offered in most of the popular stocks. As the name suggests, these options expire on a weekly schedule.

In this book, we will only trade monthly options that expire on the third Friday of each month. The reason is simple: When purchasing weekly options, although the cost is less, the time frame is so short that it's challenging to make a profit. In addition, sometimes weekly options have less trading volume.

Nevertheless, you are free to trade weekly options if that's the strategy that meets your needs. There are times when trading weekly options makes sense, but here we will only trade monthly options.

Before going on, let's look at an example of how to choose an expiration date: Let's say that it is June 8, and you want to buy calls on stock YYY. You can choose from among the several available expirations available for YYY options. As you remember, I suggest picking a date that is one to two months from the current date, which in this case would be July or August.

June 17 is the next date (the third Friday of the month), but it's too early for our methods. The next monthly expiration date is July 18, more than a month away and therefore suitable.

Hint: The longer the expiration date, the more the option will cost.

At-the-Money, Out-of-the-Money, and In-the-Money Options

Options traders use the terms *at the money*, *out of the money*, and *in the money* to describe how the strike price compares with the price of the underlying stock. By the time you finish this book, you will become very familiar with these terms.

In the following examples, we discuss only calls.

At the Money (ATM)

When the current stock price is the same, or nearly the same, as the strike price, the option is *at the money*. Therefore, if YYY were trading at $85 per share, all options with a strike price of 85 are at the money.

There is no exact definition that specifies how near to the stock price an option must be to be referred to as an at-the-money option. In other words, it doesn't have to be exactly at $85 for it to be at the money, but could be a few pennies above or below the current stock price. For example, if YYY were trading at $90.25 per share, an option with a 90 strike price is at the money.

When making a real trade, in this book we will almost always select an at-the-money option. There are a few exceptions that occur when using speculative strategies discussed in Part Two.

Out of the Money (OTM)

When the strike price of a call is above the price of the underlying stock, then the call option is *out of the money*. For example, if YYY is trading at $85 per share, calls with a 90 (or higher) strike price are out of the money. This is true regardless of the expiration date.

One of the reasons that many options traders lose money is they choose out-of-the-money options that have little chance of becoming profitable. Buying an out-of-the-money option is usually too speculative for our purposes (with a few exceptions).

> *Examples:* If YYY were trading at $87 per share, a call option with a 90 strike price is out of the money by 3 points (and a put option is in the money by 3 points). If YYY were trading at $84 per share, a call option with a 90 strike price is out of the money by 6 points.

In the Money (ITM)

When the strike price of a call is below the price of the underlying stock, the call option is *in the money*. For example, if YYY is trading at $87 per share, the next closest strike price below $87 is the July 85 call. All call options with a strike price of 85 or less are in the money.

Example: If YYY is trading at $87 per share and you chose a July 85 call, the call is 2 points in the money. If you chose the July 80 call, then it would be 7 points in the money. The more the option is in the money, the lower the strike price and the higher the option premium.

The terms described above only compare the strike price with the stock price. They say nothing about whether your trade is profitable or not. As you become more familiar with trading options, you will learn there are valid reasons for buying in-, out-of-, or at-the-money options. The main point is these terms have nothing to do with profits, only with comparing strike and stock prices.

The Option Chain

All the information discussed above is found in the *option chain*, which is a detailed list of all the options, along with their current premiums, for a given underlying stock.

The option chain contains important information that you will use when entering your option orders. Consider it as a road map loaded with vital details. Most of that information will not be of interest, but it contains everything that you need to trade options according to the methodology taught in this book. If you're new to options, you will spend a lot of time studying the option chain.

Every brokerage firm offers option chains on its website. You can also find an option chain online for any stock whose option you want to trade. After entering the name of the underlying stock, the option chain appears in order by expiration date.

As mentioned above, in addition to the expiration date and strike price, the option chain displays the stock name and symbol, the option type (call or put), and the bid-ask price.

Complex Option Concepts

Many people are fascinated by how an option's theoretical value is determined. Unfortunately, some people get so preoccupied by option theories and mathematical concepts that they lose sight of how to make money trading.

Although it's helpful to know how the mathematics of options work, it's not required. To use an analogy I used in my first book, you don't have to know how an engine works to drive a car. Therefore, you can make money trading options without a full understanding of the most complicated options concepts.

Nevertheless, below is a quick overview of two of the most important, and complex, concepts concerning options, *implied volatility* and *time value*.

Implied Volatility

It would be a mistake to teach a course on trading options without discussing *implied volatility* (IV). This fascinating but complicated characteristic is unique to options and should always be considered when buying or selling options, especially when speculating.

Right now, I'm going to give you a quick overview of implied volatility to provide a basic understanding of this concept. To fully understand implied volatility, however, consult other books, including my previous book.

Implied volatility is one of the most complicated concepts in the financial markets; yet you can still trade and make money without fully understanding how it affects the option. Nevertheless, I encourage you to make the effort. Below is an overview.

Understanding Implied Volatility

Implied volatility is a property of an option and not the underlying stock. It has a large influence on the option premium (the price at which an option trades in the marketplace).

The option premium is affected by a number of factors. These include:

1. A change in the price of the underlying stock
2. The strike price
3. The option type: call or put
4. Interest rates
5. Dividends
6. The time remaining until expiration
7. Implied volatility

An option's price depends on all seven factors above. Some are more important than others, but all these factors affect the price of an option. The first six are straightforward. However, the seventh factor, implied volatility, is the most important and least understood characteristic of option pricing.

Implied volatility is immensely powerful, and at times, it will greatly affect the price of any option. When implied volatility increases, the price of the option increases. When implied volatility decreases, the price of the option decreases.

In the marketplace prior to an exciting event such as a Fed meeting or a major financial announcement, implied volatility increases, and may even explode higher. Thus, expect to pay more for options before such events.

The bad news for options buyers is that once the event comes and goes, implied volatility, and with it the price of an option, declines. That leaves many owners of options perplexed when their stock moved higher by a point or so, but the premium of their call option declined, leaving them with a trading loss.

Therefore, implied volatility, displayed as a percentage on the option quote in the option chain, is simply what the market believes (or implies) the option is worth. It tells you how much the market is willing to pay for an option. You can determine the current implied volatility and how much it has affected the option price by looking at the option chain.

When implied volatility is high, it means that traders have a greater sense of urgency about buying the option. When options are in greater demand, premium is pushed higher. As with any investment vehicle, increased demand means that prices rise. Options buyers are willing to pay more for an option, as the underlying stock could experience a large price move in the near future.

Therefore, options that are in high demand (because the underlying stock is in high demand) increase in price, and that means that implied volatility is increasing. On the other hand, when demand for options is low, option prices, and implied volatility, trend lower.

Underlying stocks like GE or Walgreens carry a lower implied volatility (because there is less demand for the stock). It's the lack of urgency and little buying pressure on their options that causes implied volatility to be lower for stocks such as GE. The demand for these options is not as great.

By the way, higher or lower implied volatility has nothing to do with the worth of the company, but only reflects what traders and investors are willing to pay for certain options. If you find this confusing, don't worry—it is one of the most misunderstood characteristics of options.

However, if you are buying calls using the methods in this book, you will probably be trading more, rather than less, volatile stocks because those are the ones that are likely to move the most at the opening of the trading day. Those are the stocks we are interested in trading.

On one hand, you want to buy options on stocks that are volatile and move up (or down). On the other hand, you don't want to pay more than an option is worth.

Not surprisingly, options on volatile stocks cost more than those on nonvolatile stocks. Why? Because they have higher implied volatility. Therefore, it is important to understand whether implied volatility is at a reasonable level when you make the trade. If you are fortunate, you may buy options on stocks that move so high or low that the extra you pay won't be that significant (but do expect to pay more for that implied volatility).

As long as you don't overpay by too much (because implied volatility is not much higher than usual), you should come out okay. Most importantly, before trading options, it's essential to have a basic understanding of how implied volatility influences the option price.

> *Hint:* If you are day-trading options, implied volatility is far less important because implied volatility will be essentially unchanged between when you buy and when you sell the options. If you hold options for a longer time, implied volatility may change significantly as time passes, leaving you with an unexpected gain or loss.

Why Is Understanding Implied Volatility Important?

Anyone who is not aware of implied volatility would not recognize when or why an option carries a very high premium (price paid for the option). For example, instead of costing $4 or $5 per contract, the price may be $8 or $9 per contract.

Not understanding implied volatility has caused many novice traders a lot of grief. In other words, they overpay for the option because they may not have realized that implied volatility has skyrocketed. They end up buying at a very poor price.

If you aren't aware of the fair price of the option, it's easy to get burned. That means that even if the underlying stocks move in the right direction, if they don't move far or fast enough, you could still lose money. That is why millions of new traders wonder why they lost money on a trade even though the option was in the money and moving in the right direction.

They lost money because they overpaid for pumped-up implied volatility. On a typical day, when implied volatility is in a "normal" range, the option premium will be offered at relatively fair prices. But if an upcoming event causes implied volatility to move higher, then option prices will be much higher.

How do you avoid overpaying for options? With more knowledge and practice trading, you will learn what is a fair price of an option.

There may be times when you decide to pay a high premium for an option, but that is a choice only you can make. The kind of surprise you don't want is to pay too much for an option without realizing it. That's how many options buyers lose money and get disillusioned about trading.

> *Hint:* Once the upcoming event is over, then implied volatility declines, and so does the option premium.

Time Value

In addition to implied volatility, *time value* is another extremely important options characteristic because of the way it affects the option premium. Time value refers to the portion of any option that comes from the amount of time remaining until the option contract expires. Anyone who doesn't appreciate how passage of time affects an option's value is bound to lose money.

You already know that as soon as you buy an option, time becomes your enemy. As each day passes, the option price begins to deteriorate. The nearer the expiration date, the faster the option loses value.

Once you buy a call or put, the clock is ticking and the option value deteriorates. If you hold the option too long, measured in days, it will affect the profits when you own a winning option.

Why does the option lose value as time goes by? As an option approaches expiration, the underlying stock has less and less time to move in the right direction. To be specific, there are fewer opportunities for the stock to move above the strike price as the expiration date approaches.

It's the last 30 days of an option when time value becomes more noticeable. For example, if you compare a February option with one that expires in March or April, you will see that the February option is worth less because of a decrease in time value. Options with a longer expiration date (three months, for example) decay much more slowly at first. Therefore, if you buy an option with a three-month expiration date, it will erode, but not as quickly.

As the expiration date nears, options lose value rapidly. When there are only a few days left, the time value decreases even more quickly, and all time value is gone when expiration arrives.

Time value can vanish under two circumstances: when expiration has arrived or when the option is so far out of the money that it is nearly worthless. Most important: On the expiration date, an option has zero time value.

Technical note: Although the passage of time adversely affects any option premium, it is far more important that the underlying stock moves in the right direction (higher for calls and lower for puts).

Why Is Understanding Time Value Important?

Many traders lose money because they hold calls or puts too long. They don't appreciate how time affects the option price, and they keep holding a losing position, only to see its premium collapse.

Because of time value, using the strategies in this book, you will almost always choose an expiration date at least a month from the purchase date, and preferably two months. The longer the expiration date, the more breathing room you have, and the less quickly the option premium decays.

> *Note:* All the above refers to those who are buying calls and puts. If you use other strategies, such as *selling covered calls*, time is a positive factor. When selling covered calls, for example, you rent your stock to an options buyer. The covered call strategy is excellent for those who want to collect, and not pay, premium. It's a strategy worth considering when volatility is low. Selling covered calls is explained thoroughly in my first options book, and there are many other books written on this strategy, as well as many online resources.

Exercise: Your Right to Buy

If you never previously traded options, there is something important that you must know. You, as the options buyer, have the right to *exercise* the call (or put). When the call buyer exercises a call, he or she buys the underlying stock by paying the strike price.

Understand that you have the right to exercise the option—you have the right to buy the underlying stock at the strike price. It is a choice, and it is not required. In fact, you probably never will exercise an option. Using the strategies in this book, plan on selling the option when you don't want to own it any longer.

When you exercise a call, you exchange 1 in-the-money call for 100 shares of stock. You have the right to exercise at any time before the option expires, but those who do exercise almost always do so on the expiration date.

Automatic Exercise

Exercising an option may seem confusing. However, let's cut through the confusion and focus on what you need to know about this important right, that is, the right to buy the underlying stock.

First, I do not recommend holding an option until expiration. If you accept that advice, then you don't have to worry about exercise. With the strategies covered in this book, you always sell the call well before expiration, and typically on the same day, the next day, or at most one week after purchase.

If you get careless and do not pay attention, or if you are on vacation and forget that you own an option position, and fail to sell your call or put before expiration, there may be a problem. If the option is in the money by even one penny ($0.01) or more, it will automatically be exercised.

That leaves you owning 100 shares of stock (if a call option). That's the *automatic exercise* rule, and it is strictly enforced. It could even result in a margin call, forcing you to sell the stock position the next day. You don't want this to happen.

In other words, if you own any option that is in the money and you let it ride all the way until expiration, your brokerage firm will automatically exercise your option.

This means that if you owned five YYY calls at a strike price of 100, and you held it until the expiration date (and YYY closes at $100.01 or higher), those five calls become 500 shares of YYY. By the rules, you will have to buy $50,000 of the underlying stock. This is *not* a misprint.

Although your call may only be worth $5 or $10, if exercised, you suddenly find yourself owning $50,000 worth of stock. That is how a position with a small risk turns into a position with a huge risk. That is both the beauty and the danger of speculating in options.

On one hand, with only a few thousand dollars, you can control many thousands of dollars of the underlying stock. For a relatively small price, you get to participate in the upward (or downward) move of the underlying stock without investing a fortune. That's the beautiful part.

The risky part is that if you don't know what you are doing, and you allow the in-the-money option to reach expiration, and it's automatically exercised, you must pay for those stock shares. (By the way, if you own a losing option that is out of the money at expiration, it simply disappears; i.e., it expires worthless. You would owe nothing if that occurs.)

The best method for avoiding automatic exercise headaches is to sell options in a timely manner, and never hold to the expiration date. That is one reason for trading short-term options that are discussed in this book.

If you do not fully understand any of the above information, I urge you to read more books on options (mine or others), and keep practicing in the test trading account until you do understand the risk as well as the reward of trading.

The Process of Buying a Call

Now that you have an idea of basic option vocabulary, let's go through the process of buying a call in your brokerage account.

Prepare to Buy a Call

The following is a step-by-step guide to buying calls. In this example, we will use all the vocabulary words mentioned above so you can see how they are used.

1. You must open a brokerage account and specify that you want to trade options in addition to trading stocks. You should specify that you want to buy and sell calls or puts, a Level 2 strategy.

2. Let's say you are interested in buying calls on the underlying stock, YYY. When buying calls, it means that you believe that the YYY stock price will soon move higher. It's April 10, and the current price of YYY is $87.25 per share.

3. Before buying YYY, look at the stock on a chart. At first glance, you should see that the stock is in an uptrend and is moving higher. You believe that YYY will continue to move higher during the day.

4. When you look at the option chain, notice that the bid-ask prices for the option with an 87 strike price are $2.79 and $2.81. The option expires in one month, on May 18. If you bought one of these calls, it would cost $281. If you bought five calls, it would cost $1,405. Remember that 1 option contract = 100 shares of stock. *Hint*: The 87 strike price is *at the money*, meaning that the strike price is almost the same price as the stock price.

5. You could also buy one call of YYY at a strike price of 85, which is approximately two points *in the money*. Because it's in the money, it costs more to buy this call. The premium for the 85 strike price is 4.45 bid × 4.50 ask. That means if you wanted to buy one YYY call, it costs $450, the ask price (the higher price).

6. If you wanted to buy an *out-of-the-money* YYY call, it would cost much less if you buy one call at a 90 strike price. The bid and ask prices are $1.54 × $1.56. To buy one of these calls, the cost is $156. However, to make money, YYY, which is currently trading at $87.25, would have to move higher.

Advanced note: As the stock price moves higher and your call option increases in value, in-the-money options gain value more quickly than at-the-money options, which gain value more quickly than out-of-the-money options. How much an option price changes can be explained by studying the *Greeks*. The Greek discussed here is *delta*.

Buy the Call

I am certain that after you paper-trade for a few weeks, it will be easier for you to understand options. And never forget the most important rule in this book: Test before you trade.

Under no circumstances should you make a real trade with real money until you have practiced trading in the test trading account. One sure way of losing money is by buying options before you know what you are doing, and before you've been properly trained.

1. To refresh your memory: It's April 10, and YYY is trading at $87.25. Believing that YYY is going to move higher within the next few hours or days, you want to buy call options. Before making the trade, first choose a strike price and expiration date.
2. Because it is April 10, we select May 17 (which is the third Friday in May) as the expiration date.
3. Next, we choose an option with an at-the-money strike price of 87. When making a real trade, we most often choose an

option that is at the money. By choosing an option with an at-the-money strike price, even if YYY moves just a little higher, we have a better chance of earning a profit. There is no best option to trade, but for the strategies used in this book, choose an at-the-money strike price when making a real trade.

4. Now we are ready to take action. Buy one YYY call using 87 as the strike price and May 17 as the expiration date. The current cost is $2.81, for a total cost of $281.

5. When entering the order, select *Buy to Open* on your bro- kerage screen. (When you are ready to sell, hopefully for a profit, you will select *Sell to Close*.) You will buy using a *limit order*.

Hint: When making a real trade, use only limit orders. Use a *market order* only when practicing in the test trading account.

After You Press the Enter Key

As soon as you press the Enter key, the order is sent to an options exchange. Know that limit orders are not always filled immediately. Let's assume that the trade is executed and you are now the proud owner of one YYY call expiring at the close of trading on May 17. The higher that YYY stock moves, the more money you earn. If YYY moves lower, you will lose money. Because we are buying options, you want to take profits, if any, sooner, rather than later. That does not mean that you must exit the position in five minutes. It does mean you probably won't hold overnight. Using the strategies in this book, you may, on occasion, hold longer.

Now that you have made your first option purchase, the hard work begins. You should plan to monitor the option position closely and be prepared to sell the position if conditions warrant. That may mean to take profits when YYY moves a lot higher, or to cut losses when YYY moves lower.

Setting Up a Test Trading Account: Observations

Now that you know how to buy calls, continue reading the rest of the book, but first read these observations about setting up a test trading account.

1. If your brokerage firm doesn't have a test trading account (also known as a simulated trading account or a paper money account), there are a number of third-party vendors that offer test trading at no cost. It is helpful if you have access to a simulated trading account, but you can still use the strategies in this book without one.

2. The test trading account will simulate the real trading account exactly except that you do not earn or lose real money. In this book, we are using the test trading account to find winning stocks to trade.

3. Every paper money trading account is different, but you typically have the ability to set any amount in the account. Because you will make a number of test trades every day with large paper money purchases, it's best if you can set the trading amount to at least $5 million. This doesn't mean we are pretending to trade with that much money. We are only using that large amount to find winning stocks. Therefore, don't get distracted by the million-dollar paper money amount.

4. *Note*: Some brokerage firms limit how much paper money you are allowed to play with. If you are limited by your brokerage, it's not a problem, because you will just make smaller paper money purchases.

· · · · · · · ·

Congratulations on reading the first part of the options minicourse. If your only introduction to options is what you just read, your head might be spinning! Don't worry, however, because when you begin making practice trades, it gets easier, similar to the first time you drove a car.

Options Questions and Answers for Beginners

Now that you have at least a basic knowledge of how to buy options, read the following questions before continuing. The answers below should help you understand options a little better.

QUESTION: *How much money do I need to get started using the strategies in this book?*
This is one of the first questions that most beginners ask, and rightly so. To open an options account, most brokerage firms require very little up-front money. Therefore, it is not necessary to fund your account immediately.

Eventually, you need some money to trade options in the real brokerage account. In general, it's best to have at least $1,000 to $2,000 in your account when you are ready to trade. Be aware that if you have less than $25,000 in your account, the brokerage limits your account to only three day-trades within a five-day period.

If you make that fourth trade, the brokerage labels you as a *pattern day trader*, and you are required to have at least $25,000 in your account or you will be prohibited from trading with that brokerage firm for 90 days.

Even if you have less than $25,000 in your account, you can use the strategies in this book by only making three day-trades within a five-day period. It requires being more selective about the trades you make, which is not a bad thing. Therefore, do not worry if you have less than $25,000 in your account for trading. This will not prevent you from trading options.

You may wonder why FINRA (Financial Industry Regulatory Authority) established the pattern day-trading rule. The rule was approved in late 2001 after millions of new day traders had quit their jobs to become traders, only to lose most of their money when the market crashed earlier that year.

Many of these traders used margin to double the size and risk of their trading accounts. Once the market crashed, these small-time day traders discovered that all their money was gone. That's when the pattern day-trading rule was established to allow only well-financed traders to trade without limitations.

QUESTION: *How do I find the best stocks for trading options?*
This is a question asked by many beginners, and it's an important one. As you know, the universe of stocks is huge, but finding a winning stock that is suitable for options is a challenge. Many beginners turn to their friends, get ideas from financial publications, or sign on to online trading sites that recommend specific stocks.

To find your own stocks, read Part Two, where you will learn the Test Trading Strategy. There you will learn how to set up and use a test trading account to find winning stocks.

QUESTION: *Can I make money trading options every day?*
The short answer is no! People wish they could earn money every day, but it's an unreasonable expectation. The goal is to manage risk so that losses are minimal when you are wrong, and to increase gains when you are right. You want the gains to be large enough to justify the risk associated with trading. That means trading on the good days and avoiding trading on the days when risks are higher and the odds are not in your favor.

Remember that the market is a puzzle that must be solved every day. It's not just any puzzle, but similar to a Rubik's Cube with multiple problems and solutions. If you invest money in the wrong stock or at the wrong time, you will lose money.

You can't catch every twist and turn in the market, so don't even try. On some days, do not trade. Wait for the days when everything has lined up in your favor and you don't have to struggle to find good trades and make a profit. Also, don't forget that options are a wasting asset and the ticking clock diminishes profits every day. You must be willing to exit when your profit target is achieved. Trading options is very different from trading stocks. Therefore, be careful about adopting the "let winners run" strategy that is appropriate when trading non-wasting assets (i.e., stocks).

QUESTION: *How much money can you make trading options?*
This question is asked a lot. It's suggested that instead of focusing on the amount of money you could make each day or week, focus on finding a winning underlying stock, buying it at a decent price, managing the position properly, and then making a profit. The amount of profit is not as important as the fact that you made a profit.

At first, your goal should be to learn how to make consistent profits. Therefore, trying to make a profit every day is unrealistic. If you focus on making money all the time, you may make the typical novice mistake of betting too much money before you have been trained.

That's how trading options has gotten a bad reputation. At first, trade small, take less risks, and settle for fewer profits. That way, you can gain valuable experience without risking too much capital.

In addition, by trading small, you have less emotion, one of the key attributes of successful traders. You may find that the more money you trade with, the more emotional you become. That is another reason why you want to focus on being a better trader rather than focusing on how much money you can make.

Bottom line: Don't worry about how much money you want or need to make every day or every week. If you do, you are likely to overtrade, which is one of the most common ways to lose money. Another money-losing idea is to bet too much money on one trade. If you break either of these rules, stop and ask yourself: Am I trading or gambling?

QUESTION: *Can I trade options if I have a full-time job?*
This is a very common concern with people who want to trade but don't have time. The answer is no for most people. If you insist on trying, use longer-term strategies. You must also be picky about your trades, and forget about day trading. It's not fair to your employer or to your trading account to day-trade while holding a full-time job.

You can also use whatever free time you have to practice-trade, so that when you have the time, or find another job, you will know how to trade. Meanwhile, consider buying and holding stocks or index funds until you have the time to trade.

Bottom line: If you have a full-time job, keep it.

QUESTION: *I bought your book because you said I could make money trading options. I have a lot of bills to pay and need to make money fast. How do I begin?*
If you are trading because you want to make money fast, or want to get rich quick, you will be disappointed. To make money trading options requires an education, along with patience and discipline (having a set of guidelines and rules and then following them). Most importantly, it doesn't happen quickly, so trying to get rich quick is unrealistic.

It's a mistake to rely on the options market to pay bills or to buy gifts. The market is not an ATM machine. It takes a lot of work and study before you can consistently make money trading options.

I will never forget the letter I received from a 70-year-old man who said that he didn't have enough money to live on and needed to make money to pay his bills. That's why he was interested in learning how to make money quickly using options. I told him this was not a good idea, and hopefully he listened.

To be honest, some traders never make money trading options. You should know that it's hard enough to trade stocks, but trading options is even more challenging. The statistics are not favorable, and you need to know this up front.

The good news is you *can* learn to make money trading options (or I wouldn't have written this book), when you are properly trained. You cannot learn by only taking a two-day course or by just reading books (even this one). You must go out and make trades using real money, but if possible, start with a test trading account first.

> *Bottom line:* There is nothing wrong with entering the options market to make money. But don't try to use options to reach that goal fast. Take your time, learn how to trade properly, and manage risk.

QUESTION: *What is the best options strategy?*
There is no one strategy that fits all traders. That means there is no "best" strategy. Some traders like to day-trade, others are weekly traders, and some hold options longer. To find a strategy that works for you, paper-trade with a variety of strategies until you find one that you understand, and that fits your personality and trading style. Hopefully this book will give you some ideas, but don't feel pressured to use any strategy that makes you uncomfortable.

There are dozens of options strategies, some that are easy (selling covered calls or buying both calls and puts) and some that are more complex (Iron Condor, Strangles, and Butterfly).

One reason for reading this book, or others, is to learn viable strategies. Then you can choose which ones work best for you. You may find, as I did, that often the more complex a strategy, the more difficult it will be to make money, unless you are a brilliant trader with years of experience and training. For 95 percent of options traders, the simpler the strategy, the easier it will be to profit.

No matter which strategy you choose, I urge you to paper-trade before using real money. If you are already a great stock picker who is skilled when guessing market direction, you should probably stick with what you already know best. But if you are like everyone else, test before you trade.

QUESTION: *What should I do about tips that I receive from my friends?*

Most of the time, tipster stocks are nothing more than someone else's opinion. It's always better if you come up with your own ideas, although there is nothing wrong with listening. However, never buy what tipsters are hyping until you make a paper money purchase in the test trading account. The biggest mistake you can make is to blindly buy a tip stock without first testing it. Sure, the tipster may be correct. Sure, this may be a golden opportunity. But neither is likely.

By testing first, you accomplish two goals. First, you check to see if the stock tip is a good one. And second, you check to see if the tipster is reliable. That allows you to quickly determine if the underlying stock is moving in the right direction, and thus is a suitable investment. More than likely, your friend's stock idea will be as reliable as the tip sheets at a horse race.

QUESTION: *Should I buy options on stocks because of what I think will happen in the future?*

Most people are terrible fortune-tellers, and that goes for predicting which direction a stock will go in the future. Therefore, it's usually unwise to bet too much money on individual stocks or indexes based on speculation about the future.

Guess what? That's exactly what everyone does! And to be honest, making a series of bullish wagers on the stock market has paid off well much of the time. On the other hand, there are times when people lose a lot of money buying options.

If you plan to trade options, keep the trades on the small side. Betting on the future is usually a losing proposition. That is why it makes more sense to follow the market rather than trying to outwit it.

There are a few times when you can make a bet on a future outcome, but do it with a small amount of cash. These long shot trades can pay off handsomely if you are right. But if wrong, it's easy to lose your entire initial investment.

As long as you don't make too many long shot bets on a future outcome, and as long as you trade small, there is nothing wrong with making an occasional bet on what you "think" will happen in the future.

QUESTION: *Could you explain limit and market order in more detail?*

When buying or selling options, you should always use a *limit order*. A limit order means specifying a maximum price that you are willing to pay when buying an option, or a minimum price that you will accept when selling an option. If the order cannot be filled at your price—or a better price—then it will not be executed.

The only advantage of using a *market order* is that your order is filled immediately. The major problem associated with market orders is that you often get the worst possible price, which can cost you big bucks over time. With options, every penny counts, so getting a competitive trade execution is essential, which is why limit orders are preferred.

If you're in a rush and want the order filled immediately, you can submit an order to pay the ask price (the higher price) and get filled immediately. So with market orders, it's assured you will get filled fast, but not at a price that is good for you.

Bottom line: Use limit orders when trading options, not market orders.

QUESTION: *What do you mean by the bid-ask spread?*
The bid-ask spread is the difference between the bid and ask price. If the spread is too wide, then after buying, if you want to sell immediately (perhaps you changed your mind or made an error), you would lose by the difference between the bid and ask price. The tighter the bid-ask spread, the better it is for the options trader.

· · · · · · · ·

Now that you have successfully completed the options minicourse, in the next chapter, you will be introduced to basic technical analysis, which will help identify uptrends and downtrends, as well as determine when the market is overbought or oversold.

Even if you use the trading methods included in this book, it's important to have a basic understanding of technical analysis. The next chapter should help get you started.

11

Two Useful
Technical Indicators

Although you can use the Test Trading Strategy to find winning stocks, it's also possible to find these winners using basic technical indicators. Among the hundreds of such indicators, two stand out from the crowd. The reason? They are extremely powerful and easy to use.

Although every technician has his or her favorite, most agree that the two indicators below are included in the technical toolbox of almost all traders. The two basic indicators that you should learn are:

- Moving average (MA)
- Relative strength indicator (RSI)

There are a number of other popular indicators that technicians use to identify trends, entries and exits, and overbought or oversold conditions. These include VWAP, NYSE Tick, MACD, and Bollinger Bands. If you choose to further your education, there is a lot of information on these indicators in books and on the internet.

The good news is that you don't have to learn all of the indicators to be a successful trader. Just find one or two that are useful and focus on learning those.

The great thing about technical indicators is they can be as simple or as complicated as you want them to be. Keep in mind that these indicators must be viewed on a chart to be truly useful. The reason is that they provide a powerful visual that gives a quick snapshot, similar to a lab technician looking at an x-ray. Many traders, as well as investors, rely on indicators to help with buy and sell decisions, as well as to identify trends.

Moving Averages

Moving averages (MAs) are the simplest and, in my opinion, the most valuable technical indicator ever created. When put on a chart, they quickly give traders not only a visual image, but also actionable signals. In other words, moving averages will help you decide whether to buy or sell, and also will help you identify when a trend begins or ends.

For most traders, including me, before buying a stock or ETF, we first compare the stock or index price to its moving averages. That is one of the easiest and fastest ways to determine if the trend is on your side.

Richard Donchian, who developed moving averages while working at investment firms, used it with his "trend-following" system. As you know, in this book we believe in following trends, and that is why moving averages are one of our favorite technical indicators.

Moving averages show a security's price over a certain time period, such as the last 20, 50, 100, or 200 days. By overlaying the moving average on top of an individual stock or index (or ETF) price chart, you can instantly see in which direction the stock or index is headed.

If you are interested in the details, moving averages are calculated by taking an average of the last 50 days (or other number of days) of the closing price. So as the fifty-first day is added, the first day is dropped off.

In other words, old days are dropped as new days become available. The calculation is constantly moving, and the reason it's called a "moving average." By repeating this process every day, a smooth line that can be displayed on a chart is created.

Trend followers like us prefer to follow moving averages because we can quickly identify the trend's direction, as well as when it reverses. When overlaid on a chart, moving averages illustrate important information that is useful to any trader.

To see how to use moving averages, select the *simple moving average* on any stock chart. (You could also choose the *exponential moving average*, which some technicians say gives a more accurate reading.)

When the chart is displayed, it is typically the 50-day and 200-day averages that appear as the default settings. You can also add the 100-day moving average if you wish. These give a quick reading of the market direction, and if read accurately, give clues of strength or weakness.

Short-term traders, or day traders, can choose even shorter time periods. For example, some short-term traders use the 14-day or 20-day moving averages, which is ideal for very short time frames. The 50-, 100-, and 200-day MAs give a broader perspective, as if looking at the market from a distance.

Moving Average Signals

If you have never looked at moving averages on a chart before, you're in for a treat. They give a lot of significant signals that you can use in a variety of ways. For example, one of the most powerful and closely watched moving averages is the 200-day. Even investors who don't usually follow technical indicators pay attention to the 200-day moving average, and I'll show you why.

Let's start by putting the S&P 500 (SPX) on a chart. Then overlay the 50-, 100-, and 200-day moving averages. Next, compare SPX with its 200-day moving average. If SPX is above its 200-day moving average, that is a long-term bullish signal. If SPX is below its 200-day moving average, that is a long-term bearish signal.

If SPX, or the Dow, drops below its 200-day moving average, and stays below for several days, that is a signal of market weakness. At times, a short-term correction occurs after a major index falls below its 200-day moving average. When that happens, panicked traders who follow the 200-day will likely sell their holdings, resulting in further decline.

Often, after falling below its 200-day moving average, financial institutions and investors buy the dip and return the indexes above their 200-day moving averages. When this occurs, the short-term crisis is averted, and all may appear to be well.

One of the easiest and most popular strategies is based on the belief that as long as the major indexes are above their 200-day moving averages, it pays to stay long. If the major indexes fall below their 200-day moving averages, and stay below, it could be time to cash out of the market. This simple strategy has worked for decades and is one of the reasons why so many traders and investors watch the 200-day MA.

Keep in mind that it takes a lot of selling pressure to move an index such as SPX or the Dow below its 200-day moving average. Therefore, the 200-day acts as a *support level*, so if the index drops below the 200-day, and therefore below support, it's a very big deal.

The 50-day moving average is useful for short-term traders, and in fact, when the major indexes fall below the 50-day, that is an early warning sign of potential trouble.

You can overlay the price chart of any stock or index with its moving average to provide a quick and reliable way of determining whether the index or stock is on the right side of the trend.

For example, let's say you were interested in buying XYZ as an investment. The first step should be looking at its chart along with its moving average. Is XYZ above or below its moving average? If below, I would be very cautious about buying this security at this time. If above, and moving in an uptrend, it's acceptable to consider buying. Note that technicians don't usually buy just because of the results of one indicator, but typically check other indicators to confirm.

As a short-term options trader, it is far more important that a stock be in an uptrend (if buying calls), and that the underlying stock is moving in the right direction. One look at a chart will give you the answer.

The main criticism of moving averages is that they are often slow to react to market conditions. That is one reason moving averages are called a "lagging" indicator. Their signals are often late.

On the other hand, moving averages are not designed to catch tops or bottoms, but to help you identify trends. And for that reason alone, putting moving averages on a chart before buying or selling is worthwhile.

> *Note:* Another useful indicator that many traders like is MACD (Moving Average Convergence Divergence). It is a bit more complicated than moving averages, but it also provides useful information about when trends begin, end, or reverse direction. MACD is popular with many technicians, but for beginners, start with moving averages, which give quick and reliable signals.

Relative Strength Index

Relative strength index (RSI) is another simple but effective technical indicator that gives extremely useful information. Actually, RSI is an oscillator, because it "oscillates," or moves up and down between

0 and 100 on a chart. Although based on complicated mathematical formulas, RSI is extremely easy to use and interpret. Along with its cousin, *stochastics,* RSI is extremely popular with traders.

RSI helps determine whether a market or individual stock is overbought or oversold. RSI is typically displayed near the top of any chart program. If you don't see it, just select RSI from the chart's dropdown menu.

Welles Wilder, an airline mechanic and engineer, created RSI in 1976 after becoming interested in technical analysis while learning how to trade commodities.

RSI Signals

Let's start by looking at SPX on a chart (and remember that you can look at the RSI of any individual stock). If RSI rises above 70, it's a signal that SPX is overbought. Conversely, if RSI drops below 30, it's a signal that SPX is oversold.

Here's the downside, as every technician knows: Stocks and indexes can remain overbought or oversold for a long time. Just because RSI moves above 70 does not mean the stock or index should be sold. Do not expect it to reverse direction immediately. RSI is only pointing out that the underlying index or stock is overbought. If you own that stock or index, it's in the danger zone and could reverse direction, but RSI cannot tell you when. For example, I have seen RSI hit 90 on certain stocks, and yet the stock price continued climbing higher. Even though the stock was ridiculously overbought, it got more overbought.

Conversely, if RSI falls below 30, that is a flashing red warning sign that the underlying stock or index is oversold. Again, it doesn't mean a reversal is imminent, but it does point out that there was too much selling and the underlying security is due for a rally. Again, don't use RSI to time when that might occur.

Therefore, be careful about using RSI to time the market (although on occasion it does signal an imminent reversal). Instead, use RSI as a signal to alert you to when a security moves into the danger zone (30 for oversold or 70 for overbought). Obviously, experienced technicians will use it for timing purposes, but it's most useful as an early warning system.

Think of the terms *overbought* and *oversold* as more like flexible guidelines than a hard-and-fast rule. Many beginners have sold their stocks or option positions as soon as RSI hit 30 or 70, only to watch as the underlying stock got more overbought or oversold.

Personally, I have found that the major indexes such as SPX and the Dow, when hitting the upper or lower levels of RSI (70 and 30), give rather reliable signals and often alert you to an impending reversal. The timing is not always perfect, but it's reliable enough to get my attention.

> *Note:* Just as with moving averages, look at technical indicators to confirm that the security is in the danger zone and is at risk of reversing direction.

· · · · · · · ·

That concludes our discussion about the two technical indicators that every trader should learn. If you are a beginner and came here to learn the basics, you can go back to Part One and read about ways to manage risk. That is essential before you start trading with real money.

On the other hand, keep reading if you want to learn about one of the most fascinating, and successful, stock speculators in history, Jesse Livermore. No matter how many times you read about Livermore and the trading strategies he used, there is always something new to learn.

12

Lessons from Livermore

I believe you will gain insights by reading about the life of speculator Jesse Livermore and some of the trading tactics that he used. Some of his strategies worked spectacularly well, while others caused him financial harm.

The Life and Trading Tactics of Jesse Livermore

Jesse Livermore, one of the world's greatest stock speculators, became famous when he successfully shorted stocks during the 1929 crash, earning more than $100 million in a single week. It was his greatest achievement, but it ended in heartbreak and tragedy.

Livermore left home at 14 years of age to find a job at the brokerage firm Paine Webber in Boston. The owners were so impressed by Livermore's ability to solve complex mathematical calculations in his head that he was hired immediately. It didn't hurt that Livermore had a photographic memory.

After watching how stocks acted when they reached certain price levels, Livermore made his first stock trade when he was 15 years old, earning a fast $5 profit (a decent amount of money in 1892). He also observed how the firm's most successful customers made money, and created rules based on when they bought or sold stocks. It didn't take long for Livermore to get hooked on the stock market. He recorded the lessons he learned in his notebook, a ritual he repeated for the rest of his life.

Years later, Livermore used the detailed notes of his trades to publish a book about the experiences of Larry Livingston, a thinly disguised autobiography. The book, *Reminiscences of a Stock Operator* by Edwin Lefevre, became a bestseller and is still in demand today. Many of the lessons that Livermore discovered, including trend trading, were way ahead of their time, and quite controversial.

By the time that Livermore was 20 years old, he had made so much money that he quit working to become a full-time stock speculator. He started trading stocks in unregulated "bucket shops," unlicensed brokerages that were more like gambling dens than brokerage firms. At bucket shops, customers made directional bets that were booked by the shop itself rather than invested in the market.

Livermore was so successful at guessing market direction that he was banned from every bucket shop in Boston, and then in the United States. Bucket shop owners were always on the lookout for the trader they nicknamed "The Boy Plunger." Livermore often had to wear disguises to try to sneak into a bucket shop to trade.

Livermore got his nickname both because of his youthful looks and because of his strategies: When he was sure he was right, he would "plunge" into a position with all his money, earning huge sums when he guessed correctly, but in the process he damaged the accounts of the bucket shops.

Livermore stopped going to bucket shops after his life was threatened by one unsavory owner, who was not used to losing money to customers. In a way, it was a blessing in disguise because Livermore began trading at traditional brokerage firms, although he did have to adjust his strategies. He went from trading at the bucket shops to trading on the Big Board, the nickname for the New York Stock Exchange (NYSE).

An Imperfect but Brilliant Trader

Although Livermore was a gifted trader, he made many mistakes. Perhaps one of the worst was that he unknowingly crossed over from trading into gambling. This was one of the reasons why he went bankrupt three times. It was his plunging strategy, and a failure to follow his rules, that caused him the most grief.

Fortunately, each time that Livermore went bankrupt, brokerage firms with which he did business gladly gave him startup money, knowing that with his trading skills, he'd eventually recover the lost cash.

Livermore learned from his experiences that short-term trading was very unpredictable. On some days, he was wildly successful. For example, one time he turned $10,000 into $50,000 within days by betting on only one stock. Then days later, he'd lose all the gains he had just made. He often shorted stocks, which was not a popular strategy at the time.

Eventually, Livermore transformed from a day-trading scalper betting on small stock fluctuations into a longer-term trend trader.

It took years of study, but Livermore eventually learned to wait for clues that told him when to buy or sell. Sometimes the clues were hunches, and other times they were based on information that he had heard. He spent much of his time studying stock prices, which became the basis of his trading strategies.

Livermore also learned that it was important to observe the overall stock market because it also gave clues to market direction. In fact, he said that studying general market conditions was one of his greatest discoveries. In addition, instead of predicting what the market was going to do next, his former strategy, he began to look for signals that helped him decide when to buy or sell.

Livermore eventually created a "rules-based" trading system. He often said that when he followed his rules, he made money. When he didn't follow his rules, he lost money.

He made other discoveries. Livermore began to use a strategy called "pyramiding," a tactic that involved adding to positions as they advanced in price. The idea was that buying more shares of stock when your bet is winning compounds your returns.

If the stock continued to rally, and if Livermore was correct, he could substantially increase his profits. A further price increase confirmed that he was right. The compounding effect increased profits, leading to frequent huge gains.

Livermore also bought stocks after they had made a new high, a method later used by many successful investors and traders such as Nicolas Darvas and William O'Neil, among others.

One of Livermore's best ideas was to "probe" before he made an investment. Previously, he used to purchase 1,000 shares of a stock at one time. Sometimes he was right, and made money, but when he was wrong, the losses were disappointing. With the probe, he would begin by buying only 200 shares, and if proved right, he would keep adding 200 shares until he owned the full 1,000 shares.

Basically, he bought small positions at the beginning of a trade to test whether the stock was moving in the right direction. If the initial probe was successful, he would add more shares to his winning trades: buying more shares as they rallied further; shorting more shares as they continued to decline.

Livermore continued to use pyramiding and probing strategies, and they worked. On October 24, 1907, using his methods, Livermore made $3 million in a single day, shorting the market as it plunged. The only reason he stopped shorting was that the most famous banker in America, J. P. Morgan, personally asked him to stop to prevent a financial collapse. In his book, Livermore said that he felt like a "King for the day." It was his finest hour, and his reputation grew along with his bank account.

Eventually, Livermore developed a strategy where he looked for "big swings" in the market. He discovered that if he could find market leaders, the stocks that participated in strong uptrends, he could make substantial profits, and he did. He joined in the bull market of the 1920s, profiting handsomely along with everyone else.

However, in late 1928, Livermore began to believe that the market was overextended. As most people know, the market had been rising at a phenomenal pace for a decade. So when the market began to move sideways during the summer of 1929, Livermore put out probes on the short side. He paid attention when his probes began to work, even though many of them were costly.

There were many signs that trouble was brewing in the stock market. First, the leading stocks at that time had stopped making new highs, which turned out to be a red flag, although few knew it at that time. In addition, wise traders like Bernard Baruch and Joseph Kennedy were quietly selling their positions as the market continued to rally. In retrospect, the market was so overbought, there weren't enough buyers to move the market much higher.

In October 1929 the market crashed. As the value of his probes skyrocketed, Livermore plunged into the market on the short side with margin, making over $100 million in one week. Some people even blamed him for the crash because he was one of the few that had benefited. As most already know, millions of investors lost everything in the stock market, and the Great Depression soon followed.

Even after making a fortune in 1929, Livermore filed for bankruptcy for the third time in 1934, only five years after the greatest payday of his life. Losing all his money and suffering other personal problems caused Livermore to become severely depressed.

In 1940, while in the middle of a deep depression, he ordered a drink at the bar of his favorite New York restaurant, got up and went into the coatroom, and committed suicide with a handgun.

Although Livermore had once been worth millions, dated glamorous actresses, and once owned a number of large houses and boats, at the time of his death at age 63, his estate was reported to be worth less than $10,000.

The Three P's

I've studied Livermore for years, and many of the lessons he shared in his books were exceptional. At the time, trend trading was a new idea. After all, buying a stock at a high price with the intention of selling at an even higher price didn't make sense to most people, especially investors. As you know, the mantra has always been to buy low and sell high, so Livermore's ideas were revolutionary.

Livermore also studied stock prices and closely observed changes in their movement. He didn't use charts, but with his photographic memory, he was able to use his knowledge to speculate on how prices would change in the future.

There are three tactics that Livermore used, which I'll explore. I call them the three P's:

- Pyramiding
- Probing
- Plunging

As you may recall, when Livermore thought he was right about a winning position, he would keep adding to that position, not just once, but multiple times. Although the strategy sounds good, it is not without risk.

As enticing as this strategy may sound, pyramid strategies can backfire. They are especially difficult for options (as opposed to stock) traders. Because of the way that options are priced, when you pyramid, that is, keep buying at higher and higher prices, it's possible that your luck will run out (most likely because of an options phenomenon called "volatility crush"), and you'll lose much of your earlier profits.

Although the strategy worked for Livermore when he was right, his losses were substantial when he was wrong. That's why he created the second strategy, probing.

Unlike pyramiding, probing is recommended, and is a strategy that we use in this book. As you remember, it means starting with small purchases (either for real or in a paper money account). If the probe is successful, then add more shares (or contracts if trading options) until you have a full position. Probing was one of Livermore's secrets to success.

Unfortunately, when his probes turned out to be successful, Livermore used another strategy that more than likely caused him to go bankrupt multiple times. When Livermore was right, confirmed by his probes, there was nothing he liked more than to "plunge" into the market.

Plunging earned him a fortune during the 1929 crash, and it is how he became a millionaire several times over. It was also how he lost all his money. For plunging to work, everything must go right.

In my opinion, although Livermore didn't consider himself a gambler, plunging is similar to betting it all on red or black. As an options buyer, I urge you never to use the plunging strategy, and never "go all in" no matter how strongly you feel about a specific trade.

Plunging is a fast way of ending up bankrupt, and it is the exact opposite of proper risk management. I only bring it up in case you are tempted to plunge one day.

Lessons from Livermore

In addition to the lessons you learned in this chapter, there are many insightful quotes included in the book *Reminiscences of a Stock Operator*. Below, I listed three of Livermore's best, confirming that he was a brilliant trader far ahead of his time.

The Big Swing

Disregarding the big swing and trying to jump in and out was fatal to me. Nobody can catch all the fluctuations. In a bull market, your game is to buy and hold until you believe that the bull market is near its end. To do this you must study general conditions and not tips or special factors affecting individual stocks. Then get out of all your stocks: get out for keeps! Wait until you see, or if you prefer, until you think you see, the turn of the market; the beginning of the reversal of general conditions. You have to use your brains and your vision to do this; otherwise my advice would be as idiotic as to tell you to buy cheap and sell dear.

Sitting Tight

After spending many years on Wall Street and after making and losing millions of dollars, I want to tell you this: It was never my thinking that made the big money for me. It always was my sitting. Got that? My sitting tight! It is no trick at all to be right on the market. You always find lots of early bulls in bull markets and early bears in bear markets. I've known many (traders) who were right at exactly the right time, and began buying and selling stocks when prices were at the very level which would show the greatest profit. And their experience invariably matched mine—that is, they made no real money out of it. [Traders] who can be both right and sit tight are uncommon. I found it one of the hardest things to learn. But it is only after a stock operator has firmly grasped this that he can make big money.

The End of a Bull Market

And there is another thing to remember, and that is that a market does not culminate in one grand blaze of glory. Neither does it end with a sudden reversal of form. A market can and does often cease to be a bull market long before prices generally begin to break. My long expected warning came to me when I noticed that, one after another, these stocks which had been the leaders of the market reacted several points from the top, and, for the first time in many months, did not come back. Their race evidently was run, and that clearly necessitated a change in my trading tactics.

· · · · · · · ·

This concludes Part Four. If you read the book in order, congratulations for finishing. I end the book with some closing comments and additional advice. If you haven't read the rest of the book, now is the time to go to Part One, Part Two, or Part Three. Good luck!

Epilogue

Parting Words: What You Can Do Now

Congratulations for finishing the entire book! I want to thank you for taking the time to read about how to make money trading options. I hope that you learned new strategies and gained insights that you can use in the future.

Trading options can be difficult for many people, so I admire your motivation and willingness to learn new methods and ideas. Before I go, I'd like to share a few more lessons I've learned along the way.

As a freelance writer, I was fortunate to have been able to interview a number of successful traders and investors, including the late John Bogle, founder of The Vanguard Group and architect of the world's first index fund.

Bogle repeated to me his mantra that you should invest a set amount of money every month in an index fund. He also told me: "If you want, you can take 10 percent of your investment money and buy individual stocks, which is put in a separate account. I call it funny money. I bet that after 5 years, the money invested in the boring index fund will be far larger than in your funny money account."

You may wonder why a book about speculating with options includes advice from a buy-and-hold investor. In fact, Bogle's advice is wise. Before trading options, no matter how much or how little money you have, set aside a specific amount of money that you plan to use for trading.

Choosing a reasonable amount varies with each person. It could be as little as $1,000 or $2,000, or if you are like Sam and have sizable savings, limit the amount to no more than $10,000 or $15,000. If for some reason you lose that money, it would be painful, but not a disaster.

And if you do lose all that money, stop trading. You must return to paper trading in the test trading account until you figure out what went wrong and how to do better the next time.

Then trade with less and less money in the future until you can earn a profit consistently. This is not something that I made up because it sounds good. This is based on my own painful experiences and those of many others who have lost money because we didn't respect risk.

Why do you think that half the big lottery winners lose all their money within five years? It's because they didn't understand or appreciate potential risks. There may be times in your life when a huge windfall comes your way. That is when you can take 10 percent off the top for speculation (or vacations and gifts). But you must do everything in your power to protect the other 90 percent. The more money you have, the more important that you take steps to protect it.

In addition, always look for opportunities to diversify your investments. As your financial situation improves over time, when given the opportunity, make long-term plans to buy stocks, mutual funds, index funds, real estate, and/or gold (and other alternative investments), and keep some cash for emergencies.

A big mistake that traders frequently make is not moving large winnings out of their trading account and into safer investments such as money market funds or cash. If traders would simply follow this idea as they accumulate profits, it would protect them during emergencies or worst-case scenarios.

That was one of the biggest mistakes that Jesse Livermore made. When he was flush with cash at different times in his life, he failed to move cash away from the stock market. Because of Livermore's high-risk trading strategies, he should have protected himself from himself.

Before I go, I'd like to share with you a letter written by my grandfather, a successful owner of a Chicago stock brokerage firm (a *Wall Street Journal* article with similar advice was attached to the letter).

The letter contained the following financial advice setting out goals that I believe remain worthy today, although not easy for most people to achieve:

1. Begin by paying off all your debts.
2. After being debt-free, you must not be tempted to blow your money on risky financial ventures.
3. It is hard enough for most people to earn a bare living, including 95 percent who are unable to keep and acquire a fortune. This is not to discourage you but to warn you and give you courage to fight harder to be one of the 5 percent.
4. Always be prepared for the possibility that you may have to support your parents.
5. You want the privilege of helping those who are afflicted and impoverished.
6. The most important measure of success is integrity, hard work, and being right more than 55 percent of the time. This also means diversifying risks so that when you are wrong, it won't break or crimp you.
7. Never cosign promissory notes to help others.
8. Never buy stocks in small corporations to please friends— easy to buy, difficult to sell.

9. Don't be easy when it comes to lending money except in extreme cases (i.e., don't let a worthy friend down).

10. Only hard experience, proven by facts, should impress you and cause you to follow the rules just outlined.

Speaking of experience, I have learned that the best investment you can make is in people. You can't go wrong spending money on an education, a home, a new business, your children, pets, or those who desperately need your help. After all, why make money if you don't use it to improve your life or the lives of others?

Good luck trading options, and thanks again for reading my book. There is always a winning stock somewhere, and it's your job to find it. It's been a pleasure sharing my knowledge and experiences with you, and I wish that all your financial dreams come true.

If you have comments or questions about my book, feel free to send me an email to msincere@gmail.com. In addition, if you notice any errors, please let me know so I can make corrections in the next edition. Finally, if you have time, feel free to visit my website, www.michaelsincere.com.

Appendix

Where to Get Help

Here are a few additional resources that can help if you have more questions, want to pursue a more advanced options education, or learn more about the stock and options market.

Now that you finished the book, think of yourself a student of the market. That means learning as much as you can about trading and investing, and always looking for new opportunities to increase income. These resources are an excellent starting point.

Online Resources

- Email address: options@theocc.com
  The Options Industry Council (OIC), formed in 1992, is dedicated to helping individual investors, financial advisors, and institutions understand the benefits and risks of exchange-listed options. If you have questions about trading options while reading this book, you should email the OIC at options@theocc.com. The staff is extremely knowledgeable and helpful, but don't ask for investment advice. From

the basics to the butterflies, staff members will answer your questions promptly.

- Website address: www.optionseducation.org
  This is the website of the OIC, an excellent site that features podcasts, webinars, trading tools, and videos. The OIC also offers one-on-one investor services support from options professionals. All of the OIC's offerings are provided at no cost.

- Website address: www.cboe.com
  This is the website of the Chicago Board Options Exchange (CBOE), an informative site containing free options quotes, an option chain, and a calculator for determining the theoretical value of any option. It also offers online option classes, live seminars, and webcasts. The site is filled with useful educational information. It also has a convenient option chain app so you can look at quotes from a mobile device. Almost everything you need to know about options will be on this site.

In addition, the following websites contain detailed articles and news about stocks and options:

- Barchart: www.barchart.com
- *Barron's*: www.barrons.com
- Bloomberg: www.bloomberg.com
- Briefing: www.briefing.com
- CNBC: www.cnbc.com
- CNN Business: Money.cnn.com
- Fox Business News: www.foxbusiness.com
- *Forbes* magazine: www.forbes.com
- *Financial Times*: www.ft.com
- Google Finance: www.google.com/finance
- Investopedia: www.investopedia.com

- *Investor's Business Daily*: www.investors.com
- Market Chameleon: www.marketchameleon.com
- MarketWatch: www.marketwatch.com
- The Money Show: www.moneyshow
- Morningstar: www.morningstar.com
- Motley Fool: www.fool.com
- Nasdaq: www.nasdaq.com
- New York Stock Exchange: www.nyse.com
- SEC: www.sec.gov
- Seeking Alpha: www.seekingalpha.com
- StockCharts: www.stockcharts.com
- The Street: www.thestreet.com
- *Wall Street Journal*: www.wsj.com
- Yahoo! Finance: Finance.yahoo.com

Acknowledgments

To Stephen Isaacs, my editor at McGraw Hill, for his enthusiasm for the book and helping manage the project until it was completed. Also thanks to editor Noah Schwartzberg for recognizing the book's potential and what I was trying to accomplish. I also appreciate the efforts of Patricia Wallenburg for helping to create an error-free book.

The book could not have been completed without their help.

I also want to thank options expert Mark Wolfinger and author of the book *The Rookie's Guide to Options* (2nd edition). As with every book I wrote, he was willing to share with me and you.

I also want to thank options seller Warren Kaplan of Kaplan Asset Management for sharing his options strategies and insights with me, and to thank Jonathan Burton at MarketWatch for the many writing opportunities.

Finally, I want to thank the following friends for their support and encouragement: Alexandra Bengtsson, Angela Bengtsson, Nia Shalise, Harvey Small, Betsy Kagan, Sanne Mueller, Bertram Silverman, Karina Benzineb, Michael Puyanic, Lucie Stejskalova, Hazel Hall, Edith Augustine, Bradley Mann, Mike Collins, Richard F. Schäli, Evrice Cornelius, Giovanna Stephenson, and Jeffrey Bierman.

Index

About the Author

Michael Sincere interviewed some of the top traders and financial experts in the country to find out the lessons they had learned in the market so that he could help others avoid the mistakes he had made. He wrote a book about these lessons, followed by more books, including *Understanding Options* (McGraw-Hill, 2nd edition), *Understanding Stocks* (McGraw-Hill, 2nd edition), *All About Market Indicators* (McGraw-Hill), and *Start Day Trading Now* (Adams Media).

Sincere has written numerous columns and magazine articles on investing and trading. He has also been interviewed on dozens of national radio programs and has appeared on financial news TV programs such as CNBC and ABC's *World News Now* to talk about his books. In addition to being a freelance writer and author, Sincere writes a column for MarketWatch, "Michael Sincere's Long-Term Trader."

If you have questions or comments, write the author at msincere@gmail.com. You can also visit the author's website and read his blog at www.michaelsincere.com.